Workplace Wellness Strategies That Work

How to Sustain Your Company's Wellness Edge

William J. Pokluda, CEBS

ISBN – 10   0692028072
ISBN – 13   978-0-692-02807-0

Dedication

To my wife and my children: thank you for your patience, support and inspiration. And most importantly, for believing in me!

Acknowledgments

There's a famous line in the Pink Floyd song *Breath* which appears on The Dark Side of the Moon album, "All you touch and all you see is all your life will ever be." I placed this quote under my high school senior yearbook picture as a reminder to myself and others that life is a journey. From the day we are born, our lives are formed by our experiences and by the people we interact with. Conscious and unconscious stuff is tucked away in the recesses of our mind shaping our existence. You never know who or what will have an influence on the direction, quality and experience of your life. To begin acknowledging people and events that may have helped me write this book would undoubtedly and unwittingly omit someone or something of importance. Therefore, I want to thank everyone. And hopefully you know who you are!

Contents

Introduction

About 60 percent of Americans received their health insurance through their employer before the enactment of the Patient Protection and Affordable Care Act (PPACA)[1]. After the final employer mandate is rolled out in 2015 for small employers, this percentage could increase. Through this powerful and overwhelming fact, it should become apparent that employers are in a most enviable and influential position to facilitate a dramatically positive change to our health care system by offering effective workplace wellness programs. Employees are a captive audience who can become part of the solution to improve the health and productivity of our culture primarily because of their unique position and relationship to their employer.

Sounds idealistic, I know. But what if all employers offered a best-fit, highly effective wellness program to their employees and their families achieving results that most CFOs could only dream of?

I believe workplace wellness strategies can manage health care costs and increase productivity at work. Benefit costs are a significant expense to an organization. In particular, medical costs are usually the most significant (excluding retirement). To that extent, organizations should be prudent and mindful about how they go about spending such dollars that support their benefit plans.

Workplace wellness programs have gained popularity because they help organizations manage benefit costs effectively. Employers are beginning to realize employees cannot continue to sustain cost-shifting year over year. Salary increases (if offered) can't keep up with the rising cost of health care. Market practices are slowly being installed in the overall health care system, but we can't wait forever for such changes to take effect, assuming they even will trickle down. Alternative solutions are needed now.

What I propose is simple and straightforward: companies can tap into proven strategies and approaches to develop an effective approach for implementing and managing workplace wellness programs. And rather than considering benefit costs as an expense, perhaps companies can start to think about benefit and wellness costs as an investment.

Through my own professional experience, I've been fortunate enough to develop and manage a successful workplace wellness program. I've also learned about a wide range of strategies and tactics that other companies have used to manage workplace wellness. To a large extent, this book is the synthesis of experience acquired through the application of successful principles, theories and best practices that others have used before. You can benefit from the experience of those who have gone down the path of workplace wellness before you.

While many organizations offer workplace wellness programs, the question is whether they are managing them as optimally or effectively as they potentially could. It's common for companies initially offering a workplace wellness program to offer one distinct wellness program for employees, such as health risk appraisals, biometric screenings or a wellness challenge. The process to develop a comprehensive, holistic wellness strategy can take time and involve many different components that go well-beyond one or two distinct programs.

Organizations that take the time to develop a comprehensive, best-fit strategy and use proven best practice tactics will see a meaningful increase in the effectiveness of workplace wellness.

A buzzword these days is "sustainable." How can we make our workplace wellness program sustainable? Meaning, after you develop and implement the program, how do we keep it going and have it operate continuously? There is no silver bullet to answer this question. A wide range of thought and opinion already exists about how to sustain a program.

If you walked into a room of benefits professionals and asked them to define workplace wellness, there's a high probability you'd get as many responses as there were professionals in the room. The definitions may be close, but the uniqueness of their definition will be indicative of how their approach may be tailored to meet the needs of their organization. Organizations that are successful at workplace wellness didn't wake up one morning to find that they had a top flight workplace wellness strategy in place. It took time, trial and error, change management and lots of communications to get their programs off the ground.

While one size does not fit all, there are effective strategies that can help to create a "best-fit" workplace wellness approach.

Workplace wellness should be embraced as a business strategy like other cost-containment or investment strategies to improve productivity at an organization. Organizations often look for immediate or short-term results with regards to revenue and profit. This short term view is probably a reflection of the values inherent in our culture. With the right strategy, positive changes can be made to an individual's health in a relatively short period of time.

However a reduction in the total population health risk takes several years or more. Think about what it would take to turn the Titanic around. It takes as much planning and effort to reduce the total population health risk of your organization. Ultimately, it's this positive shift or flow toward healthy risk that will have long-term, sustainable impact on health care costs.

As benefit and workplace wellness professionals, we need to find a way for workplace wellness to be elevated within organizations and perceived as an effective strategy regardless of their size.
I also firmly believe that personal experience can dramatically influence and motivate behavior change.

Early in my career as a benefits professional, an employee in his mid 30's suffered a stroke unexpectedly while at work. I think all strokes are seen as unexpected until they happen, and then we all ask "Why didn't we see it coming?" An ambulance picked him up from the office and took him to the hospital. He was eventually transferred to a long-term care facility where he remained for months going through treatment and therapy. He never recovered to his normal self and today remains disabled.

While I did not know the employee intimately, it appeared that lifestyle and family health history contributed significantly to his stroke. I was troubled by this situation as I wondered what I could have done to help prevent this tragedy. Fast forward to today. Through anecdotal stories, I've learned from countless employees who have made a lifestyle change for the better. Whether it was losing weight, managing their diabetes, exercising more, eating healthier or taking advantage of prevention programs: I could tie their change back to their engagement in one of the workplace wellness programs available through work.

While organizations may still have a long way to go to enact change on a large scale, program metrics and such anecdotal stories reflect improvement which suggest that our efforts are working.

We can read or observe other organizations applying workplace wellness programs all day long, but I believe that sustainable inspiration comes from when we see the results of health care in action directly.

In 2013, I spent an evening in the emergency room of a hospital near where I live in Connecticut at the order of my doctor. I suffered a sharp pain in my chest about 4:30 p.m. during a stressful meeting at work. Given my age and health history, the doctor advised that I get checked out that afternoon. The emergency room was the best alternative at the time to get tested. While the outcome of the story got better for me, I could not say the same for most of the people who passed through the emergency room that evening.

I don't recommend that you spend time in an emergency room to gain insight into our health care system. However, the emergency room is often the place where the challenges in our health care system manifest itself.

An emergency room isn't the place for privacy either, so it's easy to observe what people are going through. After observing what other people were dealing with as they came through the emergency room, including their health situations and their treatment process, I thought about whether workplace wellness programs could have had an effect "upstream" to help them manage their health situations effectively and even prevent them from coming into the emergency room altogether.

Based upon what I saw that evening, I imagined several programs that potentially could have been designed to address their situations:

- Workplace safety classes on how to prevent and minimize injuries at work
- Promotion of mental health services (EAP) for abused women
- Self-care materials and education to treat minor cuts and scraps
- Toll-free nurse line to ask questions on symptoms, obtaining self-care treatment or even triaging them to an office visit the next morning or at an urgent care center nearby
- Lifestyle management classes to reduce risk of heart disease, stroke and diabetes

- Annual preventive visits and screenings to identify and treat conditions early
- Educational seminars to educate on the dangers of drinking and driving

…and the list could go on. As I pondered the possibilities to keep my mind off the long waiting time, I also thought about how each program would need to be tailored to specific generations, or nationalities, or work locations, or some other variable. Making workplace wellness programs meaningful to your audience may be the most significant challenge or barrier to acceptance and engagement. We need to create the vision and execute a strategy that will make a difference.

I wrote this book for several reasons.

I wanted to add value to an industry that seems to have its detractors. While workplace wellness may not always be a perfect science, it is one worthy of our support and development. It's important to have healthy dialogue and discussion over what strategies organizations can use to promote a healthy workplace. I'm not associated with a consulting firm, insurance company or wellness provider who has a vested interest in marketing their services. I've strictly approached this book from an academic point of view.

Next, I felt a professional need to document what I believe are solid practices that others can apply, learn from and develop. I've had numerous conversations with benefit professionals, some who are relatively new to the field, about how to start and implement a workplace wellness program. While there are a number of reputable books and sources on the topic, there seemed to be a need for a source that takes many of the best practices and consolidates them together.

Lastly, I like to write. What better way to express yourself than with a topic you are familiar with.

The process of writing and self-publishing a book has been challenging and time consuming. However, it's also been rewarding. I've made new professional relationships, explored new topics, and even challenged my own understanding of how the world of workplace wellness works. I encourage your feedback on what I put forth in this book. I can be found on LinkedIn as William Pokluda. You can also e-mail me at **Bill.Pokluda@gmail.com**.

Business Case for Workplace Wellness

Caring About the Health of Employees Helps Your Business

The newscaster exclaimed, "New study finds people are unhealthy. Story at 11." If most people heard this from their television, there's a good chance they wouldn't tune in unless the story delved into the shocking or embarrassing personal experiences of a famous actor, athlete or reality television star. Human nature determines why we don't want to be reminded about the negative side of our lives, especially when it comes to our own individual health.

Research shows that people are unhealthy. We don't want to believe it, but the facts are well documented and unequivocal. And our daily behaviors, lifestyle and societal practices are fueling a society that is increasingly unhealthy. The Centers for Disease Control and Prevention (CDC) reports that two-thirds of Americans are either overweight or obese. The trend is heading in the wrong direction.

Overweight and obesity

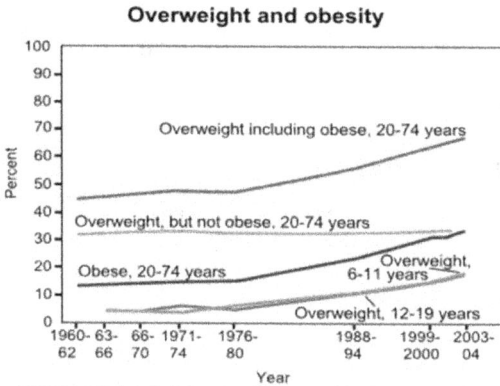

Sources: Centers for Disease Control and Prevention. National Center for Health Statistics, *Health United States, 2006* Figure 13. Data from National Health and Nutrition Examination Survey.

This particular observation was profoundly made in a documentary I watched on Netflix called *Forks Over Knives,* directed by Lee Fulkerson. The documentary illustrated, among other things, how American society transformed from an agrarian society into an industrialized nation, and as a result, our personal lifestyle along with it. Americans became more sedentary. No longer are we working on farms for hours on end to produce our own food, traveling long distances along dusty roads by foot to put food on the table, or selling our goods in a village market miles away.

One of the more significant outcomes of our industrialized culture is the increase in the popularity of processed foods, which has led to epidemic rates of obesity, diabetes and other diseases. Our culture doesn't consume the right types of food because we're influenced by our environment.

In the 1950's advertisements touted canned and processed foods to be a time-saver for busy housewives with no information ever provided about the nutritional value. Who knew it wasn't all good for you?

Inadequate physical activity, poor nutrition and unhealthy lifestyle behaviors such as tobacco use and stressful lives are all contributing toward an increase in health risk and diseases:

- Anxiety and Depression

- Cardiovascular Disease

- Diabetes

- Colon Cancer

- High Blood Pressure

- Obesity

- Osteoporosis

- …and the list goes on

People like to hear stories about how others have been affected by life's challenges. Other than the fact that humans are "rubberneckers," we also like to make correlations to our own lives, find ways to change through the inspiration (or failures) of others.

One doesn't have to look far into the past to find such inspiration, as well as strong evidence of the effect of unhealthy lifestyle behavior upon our health. I'd like to share one particularly intriguing story.

In 1977, **Jim Fixx** wrote a best-selling book titled *The Complete Book of Running* which sold over a million copies. I came across Jim's book about a year after his death in 1984 while I was training with my brother for the 1986 New York City Marathon (my first). The book was an inspiration for "weekend warriors" like me. Jim motivated us to *just do it* before Nike even coined the phrase.

Jim's book is credited with making jogging and running mainstream. However, years later his personal story is ironic. In 1984, Jim was found along the side of a road in Vermont dead from a heart attack, presumably while out for one of his runs. He had a family history of health risks. Prior to picking up running, he smoked cigarettes. He also didn't get annual physicals. There were a number of factors that contributed to his death which went ignored or undiagnosed.

For a special article published in *The Runner*, November 1984, Hal Higdon wrote about how Jim lived his life and why he died. Hal did extensive research into Jim's life and spoke with numerous medical professionals, family members and colleagues piecing together Jim's life. He asked, "Did running, in a way, kill Jim Fixx? The autopsy performed by the state medical examiner in Vermont indicated a severe case of Atherosclerosis, a form of heart disease: three main arteries showed blockage of 95 percent, 85 percent and 50 percent. It wasn't unusual that Fixx could run for so many years yet show few symptoms of the disease that killed him. "

How pervasive is heart disease? According to the **CDC:**

-About **600,000 people** die of heart disease in the United States every year — that's **one in every four deaths**.

-Heart disease is the leading cause of death for both men and women. **More than half** of the deaths due to heart disease in 2009 were in men.

-Coronary heart disease is the most common type of heart disease, killing more than **385,000 people** annually.

-Every year about **715,000 Americans** have a heart attack. Of these, 525,000 are a first heart attack and 190,000 happen in people who have already had a heart attack.

-Coronary heart disease alone costs the United States **$108.9 billion** each year. This total includes the cost of health care services, medications and lost productivity.

-Heart disease is the leading cause of death for people of most ethnicities in the United States, including African Americans, Hispanics and Caucasians. For American Indians or Alaska Natives and Asians or Pacific Islanders, heart disease is second only to cancer. For most ethnicities, heart disease does not discriminate.

-High blood pressure, high LDL cholesterol and smoking are key risk factors for heart disease. About **half of Americans** (49 percent) have at least one of these three risk factors.

-Several other medical conditions and lifestyle choices can also put people at a higher risk for heart disease, such as diabetes, being overweight or obese, having a poor diet, lack of sufficient physical activity and excessive alcohol use.

What more do we need to do as a culture to make health a priority? Our lack of sufficient action could be seen as a silent or implied acceptance of heart disease and its tragic consequences. Do we think it's acceptable to have such high rates of heart disease and death due to unhealthy behaviors in our society? Unless the health risk shows up on our door step, we usually don't pay any attention. What is the social phenomenon then that makes us believe it's the other guy who is at risk? Chances are we're already at risk, or know a close friend or loved one who is.

Dr. David Katz, Director of the Yale University Prevention Research, posted on his LinkedIn page, "Before we can ask or expect anyone to take responsibility, they must be empowered." Along these same lines, I would submit that in order to hold people accountable for their health, they need to have the tools and resources to make the change. At the very least, empowerment starts with awareness. Knowledge is power.

The business case for workplace wellness is about Jim Fixx, and the millions of other people like Jim Fixx who don't have the time, the belief system or the motivation to get and stay healthy. This is why it's important for workplace wellness professionals to understand the impact upon their organization and create a plan to help address this head on in their own organizations.

The Cost of Being Unhealthy in the Workplace

Employers are impacted by the costs of unhealthy people in the workforce either directly or indirectly. Directly, employers pay or subsidize medical costs through insurance premiums or self-insured payments. Financially, the purpose of insurance is to reduce the cost of medical care to individuals. Insurance health risk is spread out across large groups of people to minimize the burden on any one person. According to the Kaiser Foundation 2013 survey, employers typically pay 50 percent to 75 percent of the cost of premiums with employees picking up the rest through payroll contributions and/or out-of-pocket costs such as deductibles, co-pays and coinsurance.

Historically, insurance came about to help offset the cost due to an unexpected illness, injury or accident. Today, it's estimated that nearly 60 percent to 70 percent of medical costs are the result of unhealthy lifestyle behaviors, such as tobacco use, lack of exercise, poor nutrition and obesity. It's estimated

that a morbidly obese person can have higher health
care costs by about $5,530 annually.

Non-Retiree

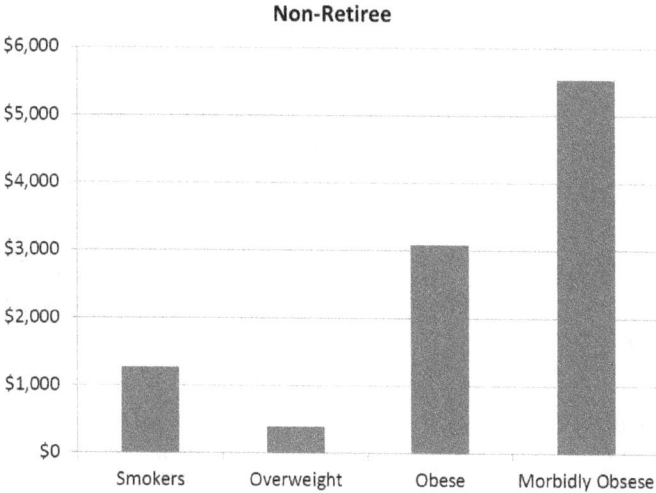

Source: Moriarty, J.P. Branda, M.E., Olsen, K.D., Shah, N.D.,
Borah, B.J., Wagie, A.E., Egginton, J.S., Naessens, J.M. (2012).
The effects of incremental costs of smoking and obesity on health care
costs among adults: A 7-year longitudinal study. Journal of
Occupational & Environmental Medicine, 54(3), 286-291.

Imagine if you could reduce the number of obese and smokers in your organization by just 10 percent. Using the estimates in the Financial Savings Model chart, a company with 500 adults (assuming only employees and spouses) could potentially reduce their health care costs by nearly $109,000 in the first year. This could be a way to find support for funding your wellness programs.

Health Risk to Change	Change 10% of Potential Population	Annual Savings in First Year After Change
Smokers *CDC estimates 20% of Americans use tobacco products*	20% of 500 = 100 10% x 100 = 10	10 x $1,274 = **$62,700**
Obese to Overweight *CDC estimates 30% of Americans are obese*	30% of 500 = 150 10% of 150 = 15	Reducing obese to overweight 15 x $2,704 = **$40,560**
Overweight to Normal Weight *CDC estimates 30% of Americans are overweight*	30% of 500 = 150 10% of 150 = 15	Reducing overweight to normal weight 15 x 382 = **$5,730**
Total Savings		$62,700 + $40,560 + $5,730 = **$109,000**

Conservatively, for a medical plan with 300 employees (or a total of 1,000 members which includes dependents) the total annual medical spend could be about $2,000,000. Therefore, reducing the number of smokers and obese population by just 10 percent could save 5 percent on your trend. Normal health care trend these days before plan design changes is estimated at between 7 percent - 10 percent depending on your industry and other factors. You could be seen as a hero.

Reducing health risk and associated costs is almost like creating art. There are so many influencing factors, but the evidence suggests that specific health factors and behaviors carry more health costs. Nevertheless, it's only logical that reducing those health risks will put an employer in better financial position.

Presenteesim: The Silent Influence on Health Care Costs

One of the more pervasive, detrimental and least understood influences at work that increases the costs of health care is presenteeism. Defined as being physically present at work, but not performing duties at full capacity due to illness and various distractions, presenteeism is estimated to represent 61 percent% of the total cost of an employee at work.

Average Annual Cost Per Employee 2010

	% of Total	Cost
Presenteeism	61%	$10,122
Sick Leave	5%	$1,737
Workers Comp	2%	$672
Disability	3%	$1,111
Health Plan	29%	$21,256
	Total Cost	**$34,918**

Source: Goetzel, JOEM, (2004) data adjusted to 2010 by Mercer Employer Survey Results and by Collins Presenteeism study (2005) of Dow Chemical that was used for determining Presenteeism cost.

Employees who report for duty while they are still sick or distracted with family and personal matters are less productive. The distraction is stressing them out, preventing them from being on-the-job 100 percent. This also impacts others on their team or managers who need to pick up the slack as the work still needs to get done, or worse yet, workers unable to perform their job with no one else there to pick up the slack. This translates into less than ideal productivity levels.

Employees continue to come to work sick or remain distracted for a host of reasons:

- Insufficient sick and/or leave time available
- People need the money
- Sense of duty
- Commitment
- Disappointing their fellow co-workers
- Fear of losing their job

Presenteeism, however, is a hard concept to see, touch and measure. It requires organizations to measure the impact of lost work time. Regardless, organizations attempt to offer solutions because they readily observe and appreciate when an employee is struggling with personal issues. The direct consequence can be an impact on productivity at work. Intuitively, you know that if an employee doesn't come to work, you have a productivity opportunity to address. Who else is going to handle the responsibilities?

Organizations offer a variety of ways to mitigate the concept of presenteeism. You may already be offering these without actually labeling them as such.

Offering health and wellness programs and services that are more readily available to people:

- Onsite health services
- Telemedicine
- Onsite gym or fitness center
- Onsite lactation support
- Ergonomic workstations and resources
- Onsite child care services

Providing an employee assistance programs (such as an EAP) that can help employees be effective in all areas of their lives:

- Child care or elder care services
- Educational / counseling services to reduce stress
- Personal financial or legal support

Establishing work/life policies that provide the structure and organizational support to enable employees to be more productive in ways that are meaningful to them:

- Work from home (telecommuting)
- Flexible work schedules
- Work-sharing programs
- Paid time off/vacation policies
- Additional time off to obtain annual health visits
- Leave or disability programs (FML)
- Concierge services (dry cleaning, administrative support, transportation)
- Tobacco-free worksite or campus

Leadership within an organization can have a significant impact on productivity and presenteeism. Leaders can show by example, provide cultural cues demonstrating their acceptance and support of these programs.

Overall, the financial and organizational reasons for having workplace wellness programs are evident.

Develop an Annual Planning Process

Organizations are in a unique position to help people with workplace wellness. Not only does it have a fiduciary responsibility to be engaged, but the organization can serve as a vehicle or platform through which employees address their health. But what can they do to address the need and how do they even start?

If you've already begun offering workplace wellness programs, then you're in a good place. You have a foundation to build upon. If you're just beginning to explore or expand upon workplace wellness, then you're at an even more exciting place.

Either way, it's important to have a game plan, an approach to your programs that you develop and review annually. Your approach says a lot about your commitment to workplace wellness. A formal game plan toward workplace wellness will naturally force you to improve and enhance upon what you offer, as well as raise visibility and accountability for workplace wellness programs. The end result should be improved employee health.

Cycle of Wellness Program Management

Strategy
Start with defining your scope. What do you want to accomplish and over what time frame? Be realistic.

Planning
Create a picture of what your programs will look like, the timeframe you need to implement, which needs to be aware and an assessment of your current programs, resources and needs.

Resources
Who is going to deliver and manage workplace wellness programs? Will it be you or others in your HR/benefits team, employees or vendors? Or are you the sole person to manage the programs?

Metrics

What type of data do you need to support decisions to invest in programs? How will you measure and track progress? What has been your historical experience up to this point?

Implementation/Execution

Making the time to walk the talk; putting things in place. Project management skills are often critical in this component. Do you need to balance implementation of other organizational programs?

Communications

What will you need to effectively communicate your program, motivate and engage your employees? Do you need to develop your own campaign, materials and tools? Do you have the skills to write an e-mail, direct mail piece, posters, PowerPoint presentations, blogs, and intranet content? Do your health and wellness vendors have materials they can offer up? Have you developed a timeline to manage?

Program Evaluation/Feedback

What's working, what's not? Do you need to change course mid-year? How do you advance your program further next time based upon results and experience on the first go-around? What insights can your vendor provide? Did you do a survey to obtain participant feedback?

Use a Common Frame of Reference

A starting point for any reasonable discussion on a topic is a common frame of reference or set of principles. The field of workplace wellness has a number of "frames of reference" that many organizations use. Think of it as a moral compass, a beacon, a true north or set of principles to steer your decision process. Using a common frame of reference allows us to put workplace wellness into an easily understandable perspective enabling us to validate our programs and strategy.

Six Dimensions of the Wellness Model

The National Wellness Institute based in Wisconsin promotes the Six Dimensions of the Wellness Model. Created by Dr. Bill Hettler, co-founder of the National Wellness Institute, each of the six dimensions are interconnected in some holistic way. This model is a great place to start because it addresses the very reason workplace wellness exists: the individual person.

The model helps to understand and apply wellness to a person's life and see how they view what's important to them.   Workplace wellness programs need to be developed for the person in a way that is meaningful to them, otherwise it won't work.

Wellness Dimension	Example
Physical	Cardiovascular, weight, blood pressure, nutrition, fitness, stress
Social	Groups, hobbies, connection
Emotional	Love, intimacy, support
Intellectual	Education, academic
Occupational	Career, job, paycheck
Spiritual	Religion, church, praying

Dean Witherspoon, President and Founder of Health Enhancement Systems, shared with me his opinion on what he thought are the top challenges that organizations face when communicating workplace wellness to employees. For over 20 years, Dean's company has been helping organizations develop wellness campaigns and facilitate behavior change.

Dean conveyed, "The only way to cut through is to make it completely relevant to the audience. That is accomplished by understanding what employees and their family members care about. In other words, I'll only care about what you have to say if I believe you care about me." This speaks volumes as to why you need a frame of reference. What kind of wellness programs should you offer? What kinds of programs are meaningful to your employees and their families?

Population Health Management and the Health Care Continuum

The concept or field of study called Population Health Management (PHM) is a popular and effective way to develop a frame of reference to manage workplace wellness.

From a purely academic perspective, PHM is defined as the health outcomes of a group of individuals, including the distribution of such outcomes within the group. The field of Population Health includes health outcomes, patterns of health determinants, and policies and interventions that link the health outcomes of a group and their distribution. [13]

In this definition, "groups" of individuals are categorized together by common health attributes. This makes it simpler to understand their unique needs and develop targeted programs to improve their health, if needed. Health status can fall along a continuum where you have the idealized healthy or well-being on one end, and the catastrophically ill on the other end. The following graphical representation published in The Art of Health Promotion helps to put PHM initially into perspective.

The Health Care Continuum

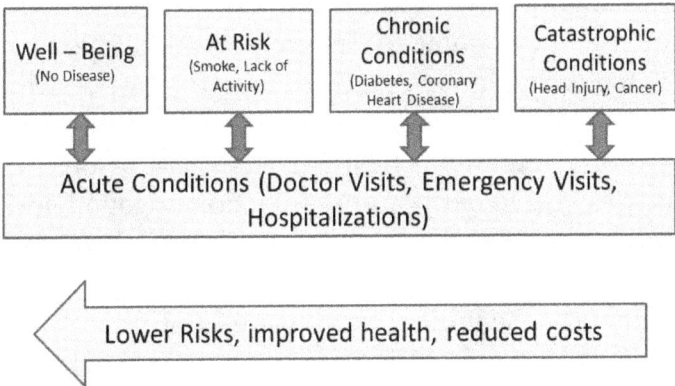

Well – Being (No Disease)	At Risk (Smoke, Lack of Activity)	Chronic Conditions (Diabetes, Coronary Heart Disease)	Catastrophic Conditions (Head Injury, Cancer)

↕ ↕ ↕ ↕

Acute Conditions (Doctor Visits, Emergency Visits, Hospitalizations)

◁ Lower Risks, improved health, reduced costs

One observation to make here is that low-risk individuals who stay low-risk continue to have low costs, but low-risk individuals who become high-risk have costs equivalent to the costs of those with high risks. Other than offering competitive benefit packages, employers are driven by balancing these programs in a cost-effective manner. It's in an organization's best interest in many ways to invest in health and wellness programs as a strategy because of the potential impact on the overall employee (and related family) population.

Another insightful and practical lesson to take from PHM is it allows you to easily develop a comprehensive approach to designing and implementing workplace wellness programs. While you may not be able to design it overnight, you can strategically plan over a three to five year period programs to implement that cover the full spectrum of your population's health needs. As a result, this enables you to get your organization engaged and moving in the right direction.

If you take the initial Health Care Continuum graphical representation a bit further, you get to drill down deeper into each of the different groupings or categories along the continuum, thereby identifying specific workplace wellness programs and plan design initiatives that can be included in your long term approach.

Comprehensive Population Health Management Program Framework

Well – Being (No Disease)	At Risk (Smoke, Lack of Activity)	Chronic Conditions (Diabetes, Coronary Heart Disease)	Catastrophic Conditions (Head Injury, Cancer)

⇕ ⇕ ⇕ ⇕

Acute Conditions (Maternity, disability, self-diagnosed conditions, strains, sprains, colds)

Health Promotion	Health Risk Management	Chronic Disease Management	Disability Management	High Cost Care Management

Health Advocacy Alignment of Services, Communications, Measurement and Evaluation

Source: *The Art of Health Promotion May/June 2006,* Best Practices for an Integrated Population Health Management (PHM) Program. Seth Serxner, PhD, MPH, Steven P. Noeldner, PhD, and Daniel Gold, PhD.

"Recycling" as an Analogy Applied to Workplace Wellness

The business case for workplace wellness contains elements of altruism, and I liken it to the concept of recycling.   To a certain extent, organizations are motivated by their own self-interests primarily because of the competitive landscape and are not concerned about the welfare (generally) of their competitors or general industry.

As we're all aware, organizations compete on many levels: they want to offer the best product; offer the most competitive price for their product; offer the best value; earn high satisfaction levels; and obtain customer loyalty.

However, one area that organizations compete in that has become an extremely hot topic of late is the "war on talent" — finding the right talent to help grow and expand the business. I also believe the concept of talent is central to my analogy of "recycling" to as it applies to workplace wellness.

Go with me on this one!

Today, most employees are not tied to an organization for life. The median number of years that wage and salary workers had been with their current employer was 4.6 in January 2012, according to the U.S. Bureau of Labor Statistics. This measure, referred to as employee tenure, was higher than the median tenure (4.4 years) in January 2010.

There's a natural rate of turnover in the employment industry for a number of obvious and acceptable reasons. In addition to downsizing, which is driven by employers, a recent nation-wide employee survey conducted by Kenexa in 2011 identified a number of reasons why employees leave an organization. The list includes: the lack of (career or professional) opportunity, inadequate compensation, lack of challenges, poor work/life balance and job stress.

According to the U.S. Department of Labor's Bureau of Labor Statistics (BLS), the average turnover rate in the United States is 3.1 percent. (Oct. 2013). This doesn't count layoffs, downsizing and discharges. Therefore, the rate of employees leaving an organization is presumably higher. Companies are still hiring employees, though. They are backfilling positions created by employees who quit, they are creating new jobs due to growth and expansion plans, and they are hiring employees because of retirement.

In January 2014, I did an informal internet search to list all open jobs posted to CareerBuilder.com. My search resulted in 100,000+ postings. According to BLS, employment in the United States is projected to grow 10.8 percent from 2012 to 2022, adding 15.6 million jobs.

The point is there's a natural exchange of talent flowing between companies at any given time. And most of the time, employers are hiring from generally the same pool of candidates in a geographic area. Over the course of an employee's professional career, they will work for many different companies.

In my recycling analogy, overall health and wellness is what we consider "waste." I don't mean to infer that people are waste. On the contrary, they are a huge asset. However, when you and I separate out plastics, paper and other recycling materials from our general garbage, we're contributing to the overall "good" to keep our planet clean and healthy. However, the concept is a tough one to get because you don't see an immediate effect or receive immediate gratification from recycling. You "feel good" about the experience and hope that in the big picture it's helping.

Health care is becoming a much more relevant concept shared by all organizations, primarily because of the rollout of PPACA. Employees carry with them their particular health status when they go to work for a new employer. Besides bringing their skills, talent, education and years of experience to the job, they are also bringing their personal life with them.

Take, for example, an employee named Bob. He's been working for a company for over four years. Bob's company really isn't offering a comprehensive or effective workplace wellness program following a Population Health Management approach or using any other strategy. During that four year period, Bob never got an annual physical, was under lots of stress and rarely exercised. Plus, he smoked cigarettes.

Then, one day Bob decides to leave his company for another employer offering him a better position with better opportunities. Bob's new employer inherits his health status as Bob enrolls in the employer's medical plan. Bob's new employer begins to include him into their "population health management" pipeline and bear the costs and opportunities that are associated with him, as well. They identify how his body has suffered as a result of his lack of exercise, high stress level and his increased risk for heart disease because of his unhealthy lifestyle.

On the flip side, if an employee leaves an organization who had a well-run, state-of-the-art workplace wellness program after reducing their level of health risk significantly, that new employer will inherit a healthy employee with low health care costs.

What if all organizations operated with comparable workplace wellness strategies? What if there was an equal sharing of responsibility to provide effective programs that kept employees healthy and helped to reduce their health risk? What if there was a mutual appreciation, understanding and action taken toward making the health of employees (and their family's health) a priority?

The concept of recycling as applied to workplace wellness programs indicates that all employers have a responsibility to do what's right.

One of the objections or challenges rose by organizations when considering whether to implement workplace wellness programs (perhaps primarily by smaller sized companies), is that their medical plan is fully-insured. The medical premiums are set by the medical plan, either through some type of community rating or blend of underwriting and community insurance rates, when they are fully insured. The premiums are determined by the overall risk level of the entire risk pool or group, along with some factor for administration and profit. As a result, the smaller organization may not see the incentive to invest in workplace wellness programs because they may not believe they can modify their premiums if they lower the health risk of their employee population.

In addition to the altruistic concept of "recycling" talent, organizations need to rise above the pure financial motivator and consider the overall impact of workplace wellness programs on the culture of the organization and the productivity their employees.

A Brief History of Workplace Wellness

Decade	Trend	Focus
1970s	Fitness	• Jim Fixx • Presidential Sports Award (President's Council on Sport, Nutrition and Fitness)
1980s	Risk Reduction	• Chronic Disease Management
	Health Productivity Management	• Linking health, productivity and profit
1990s	Population Health Management	• Focus on every phase of healthcare continuum
2000s	Sustainability	• Aligning HPM & PHM with company business strategy
2010's	Outcomes	• Participation / Consumerism • Influencing outcomes and behavior change

Behavior, Motivation and Engagement

Engage seems to be one of the more prevalent concepts companies are challenged to aspire to when it comes to workplace wellness. Companies need employees to be "engaged" in one or more of their workplace wellness programs in order to make positive change their behaviors, such as healthy lifestyle changes. For many companies, being engaged also means using a wide array of online tools and information to make better financial decisions about the direction of their use of health care (consumerism).

In the quest to communicate with and engage employees, things still boil down to how to frame the message around "what's in it for me." What is the benefit to the employee if they engage in a wellness program? For population health management approach, the bottom line is to keep employees on the side of positive health or to guide them toward the healthy side of the spectrum (reducing their risks).

But motivating employees isn't easy. I think most
of us would be happy if employees just started to
participate in one or two key wellness activities, let
alone eat their five fruits and vegetables every day.

Behavior is Difficult to Change

Drivers of Behavior
In the field of psychology, scientists believe there
are several main drivers of behavior. The first being
biological which comes from within. Thirst, hunger
and the need to satisfy other carnal urges are
examples of such internal drivers.

A second driver of behavior comes from our
environment — rewards and punishment. Rules of
law, social norms and the pirate code are examples
that guide behavior toward a particular outcome.
Studying hard to get an A in school, praying for
good things to occur and being nice to your sibling
in order to get gifts at the holidays are also
examples of the environment motivating us to
behave in a certain way.

Extrinsic type rewards are prevalent in employer workplace wellness programs, primarily because they are simple to implement and measure. We see them in practice as financial rewards, gifts and other recognitions. The delivery mix of extrinsic wellness incentives are often referred to as "carrots and sticks." Are you providing a positive reward for participating or performing in a wellness program like a payroll reduction? Or are you providing a negative consequence for non-compliance such as higher payroll contributions?

Motivating employees to engage in wellness programs and improve their health can be delivered in many shapes and sizes. There's much debate over whether to use a carrot or stick approach. In reality, the jury may still be out on this topic, but a combination or a mix of approaches is probably a good strategy. Organizational cultures need to find the right balance of extrinsic motivators that work best for them as there are both opportunities and challenges for both. Organizations need to send appropriate messages (direct and indirect) to their employees concerning wellness program incentives. How do we balance the fine line between incentivizing people to change their health and just providing the resources?

Extrinsic rewards do motivate people. But they motivate people to *get* rewards, not necessarily to change their behavior for the long term[5] which is the more sustainable and noble objective. People will work only to the point that triggers the reward, no further. If you reward people to exercise, stop smoking or take their medicines, you'll probably get great results initially. However, the healthy behavior disappears once the incentives are removed.

Intrinsic Motivator of Behavior
Behavioral scientists discovered a third driver of human behavior. "Intrinsic motivation" is driven by an interest or enjoyment in the task or behavior itself, and exists within the individual rather than relying on external pressures or a desire for reward.[5] From a health perspective, people are motivated intrinsically because they want to make improvements for personal reasons. As a result, they tend to sustain that behavior change for the long term.

Workplace wellness professionals designing programs need to be realistic when it comes to changing behavior. You never know when that moment will come when a person says "it's time for a change." Until that moment arrives, an organization needs to offer workplace wellness programs as if they were assembling scaffolding or infrastructure of a building.

Science tells us that eating right, exercising and reducing lifestyle risk leads to longevity and better health. A workplace wellness strategy needs to encourage employees to do the right thing. It's important to understand the levers that will motivate human behavior to the point where intrinsic motivation takes over.

Use Financial Incentives with a Purpose

Let's Face It, Money Talks.

Across the board, companies have been increasing the breath and value of financial rewards to incent employees in health and wellness programs. Companies have also expanded the use of financial disincentives and designed tighter consequences for not participating or engaging in health and wellness programs. While we can wait for people to become enlightened and be motivated intrinsically, most companies don't have the time or patience to do so. As a result, they need to offer ways to motivate employees to get engaged.

In 2013, more than two-thirds of all companies were expected to offer some type of financial incentives in 2014, up from just over one half in 2010.[6] One of the main drivers for the rise in financial incentives is the positive response by employees to participate in such programs when money is available.

However, there are a number of other underlying reasons fueling employee participation in wellness programs:

Increase Cost Sharing To Employees
Employees are looking to take advantage of earning extra money to help lower their payroll contributions or help fund out-of-pocket health expenses. Employers are shifting a greater share of health care cost-sharing onto employees. Generally, employees are paying about the same percentage of monthly premiums that they have over the past few years. However, their monthly premium has increased over the same period. Kaiser Family Foundation Employer Health Benefits 2012 Annual Survey reported that the annual premium cost for health benefits increased over two and a half times from 1999 to 2012. Even though the employee percentage of the total cost remained nearly the same, their overall share of the total cost has increased significantly.

Enhanced Measurement Capabilities

Incentives have gained traction because of an increased ability by employers, health plans and vendors to measure and report on a wide range of wellness program activities, thereby increasing visibility to employees. Enhanced systems and processes behind the scenes make it easier to report on participation. Reporting can be used to impact payroll contributions more easily and timely.

Availability of Industry Data

Benchmarking and industry reporting on the best practices of wellness programs has gained more visibility. Companies want to offer what successful companies are offering, including that of their peers. Many companies did not want to be "early adopters." They waited on the sidelines to see what experience would tell them. However, benefit brokers and consulting firms are more adept at modeling out wellness programs with ties to financial incentives, illustrating how such strategies can help minimize the growth in the health care trend, at least theoretically.

Benchmarking by Companies

Companies also want to be like their peers. News articles, studies and survey results are published more frequently highlighting the use of financial incentives. I remember how hard it was about six years ago to get approval just to reward employees (let alone spouses) $50 for completing their health risk assessment. Today, the question is no longer whether we should incent, but how much to reward.

Financial Incentives are Working

Directional evidence suggests that employees are coming to the table and participating in wellness programs. According to OptumHealth, on average, 49 percent of eligible employees participate in company wellness programs, significantly more than the 42 percent participation reported in previous years, with small companies having a higher average participation rate than large ones (61 vs. 45 percent).

One of the key drivers influencing employees to participate is financial incentives. An ongoing benefits survey by Towers Watson estimated that use of incentives by large employers for participating in programs grew from 36 percent in 2009 to 80 percent in 2012.

Consensus in the industry is that financial incentives cannot be the only tactic you use to motivate employees and help them sustain behavior change. It's important to use incentives wisely, and apply according to what makes sense for your organization. Employees at different levels of the organization may view a financial reward for completing wellness programs different than others. After implementing financial rewards for participation as a "carrot" approach, you may have to transition over time to more of a "stick" approach to generate participation and change by a larger portion of your employee or member population. Financial incentives are ideal to increase short-term adherence to behaviors like participating in an exercise program, tobacco cessation or completing a health risk assessment. When the incentive is seen as hefty enough, money will motivate employees to participate in a specific activity in the short-term.

In actuality, financial rewards can backfire because employee behavior is supported by an extrinsic or external financial incentive. If you take the incentive away, the behavior will most likely stop. There is very little evidence that financial incentives can change behavior for the long term. Evidence does suggest, however, that incentives can shift the source of a person's motivation from self-improvement to just earning the incentive. [8]

In the long term, their underlying behavior won't change unless there is more of an intrinsic or personal reason to change. According to the Centers for Disease Control, the quit rate on smoking is under 10 percent. People often try more than five times to quit before they actually do. This doesn't mean you shouldn't provide financial incentives. You should, however, keep incentives in perspective and not let the financial "carrot" be the essential or main ingredient to get your employees motivated.

A Few Words from the Wise

Financial Incentives May Only Represent 10 Percent of the Equation

Michael P. O'Donnell, MBA, MPH, PhD Editor in Chief, *American Journal of Health Promotion* wrote in an editorial in the Jan/Feb 2014 issue titled *Huge "Wellness Incentives" Are More About Health Plan Benefit Design Than Health Promotion.* His concern, to which I whole heartedly agree, is the Patient Protection and Affordable Care Act's impact on health plan design that went into effect in 2014, increasing the amount of wellness incentives that an employer can offer. Such incentives can be embedded or added into the total premium or costs of a medical plan which are then shared in part or in whole by employees.

Dr. O'Donnell estimated in his editorial that financial incentives are 5 percent to 10 percent of the total (workplace wellness) solution to motivate behavior change. His work over the past 30 years has shown that programs are most successful in engaging employees, improving health, reducing medical costs and enhancing productivity when they concentrate in four basic areas:

Increasing Awareness
Helping employees to understand the link between lifestyle and health outcomes and to realize they can be successful in enhancing their health and the quality of their life through lifestyle change.

Enhancing Motivation
Motivating people to be interested in improving their health is probably the second most important step. Employers can do this by treating each person as a whole human being with many priorities beyond health, engaging employees in the process of developing and implementing the program, marketing programs with effective communication, utilizing a combination of extrinsic and intrinsic incentives, providing effective senior management and program-level leadership, tailoring programs to individual needs, offering effective programs, ensuring the confidentiality of all personal information, and conducting health assessments to measure health status.

Building Skills
Building skills is probably the third most important step. Help people develop the skills they need to practice a new health behavior. While goal setting and tailoring programs to meet an individual's needs are critical, learning how to integrate new behaviors in to one's life is probably just as important.

Creating Opportunities

The most important factor is probably creating opportunities to practice these positive health habits by shaping, leveraging or overcoming the forces in the environment that influence most people's behaviors. These include:

- the influence of peers, coworkers and other friends
- norms in their places of worship, schools their children attend, social clubs, grocery stores, fitness centers, and the other places they play and relax
- laws at the local, state, and national level
- trends in society
- the built and natural environment
- challenges and opportunities caused by socioeconomic status.

Use Financial Incentives to Get Employees on the Wellness Bus

The goal of the incentive program should be to get people "on the wellness bus." Ultimately, an employer wants employees to take part in its program and adopt healthier behaviors because they are intrinsically motivated to do so. In an article for *Benefits Magazine,* [9] Kristie Zoeller Howard, CEBS highlighted five key takeaways you should keep in mind with respect to financial incentives for wellness programs:

1. Reward programs are more likely to convey a sense of cooperation between employer and employee.
2. Employers need to offer rewards that are valued by most participants: cash, merchandise gift cards and benefits-integrated incentives are most popular.
3. Tying the incentive to health plan contributions or benefit design is a cost-neutral approach that communicates the link between healthy behavior and the cost of health care.
4. "What's in it for me?" — the benefits of exercise, for example — should be emphasized

to wean employees from incentives and foster long-term behavior change.

5. Incentives based on outcomes bring with them additional regulatory requirements and may result in backlash from employees. Employers that consider offering them should be cautious.

Stratify Incentives

Aon Hewitt reported in their 2013 Health Care Survey [10] that while employers are identifying increased participation in health and wellness as a high strategic outcome, the biggest challenge or obstacle is motivating employees to change. Financial incentives are a key mechanism to help facilitate that change. Employers are taking a fundamental and calculated approach to how financial incentives are used. To understand this approach, it's important to view how financial incentives are offered in three distinct categories:

- Completion or Awareness Rewards. Eighty three percent of employers offer a financial reward for one-time activities like completing a health risk assessment, biometric screening, consumer tool or health webinar.

- Taking Action Rewards. Fifty six percent of employers incentivize employees for active participation in health programs such as wellness campaigns, health coaching and disease management.
- Achieving Outcomes Rewards. Twenty four percent of employers are offering rewards for the attainment of specific clinical values or quantified progress in health metrics like reduction in BMI, blood pressure and cholesterol levels.

More employers are requiring participants take a more active role in their own health care planning. Aon Hewitt continued to report an increasing trend by employers to inform employees about their health risks and inspiring them to change behavior. The goal is to link employee behaviors — and increasingly, access to health benefits — to positive outcomes. This is the next step in the evolution of incentives which supports a Population Health strategy approach.

Behavioral Economics

An academic field of study gaining popular interest with benefit professionals is Behavioral Economics. Blending principles from psychology and economics, behavioral economics explores how individuals make choices in complex contexts, such as personal finances and health, and seeks ways to improve their decisions and behaviors.

When applied to benefit plan design and workplace wellness, the field of behavioral economics can help to understand how people can be "nudged" toward making better decisions that benefits themselves, as well as the organization.

The heart of this approach targets people who often make decisions that are irrational or not based upon facts and showing how knowledge can benefit them directly. For example, most people understand the need for preventive health care as a way to identify and treat health risks early. They also appreciate how many health plans cover preventive care screenings without deductibles, copays or coinsurance (thanks to Obamacare). However, most people don't get health screenings.

Behavioral economics as applied to benefit plans and workplace wellness aims to help define clear choices for people through proactive, vivid communication messages that convey the value of making smart choices. There's an assumption that people read what we send them, and that they are well-informed. However, on the contrary, most of us don't read our benefit communications or fully understand what our options are.

While this is brief overview of behavioral economics, I am by no means an expert on this topic. I encourage you to research the field of study and learn how other organizations are applying the principles. Here are several great resources where you can learn more:

Reducing Suboptimal Employee Decisions Can Build the Business Case for Employee Benefits.
Benefits Quarterly; Vol. 29 First Quarter 2013, Steven F. Cyboran, CEBS, Sibson, Christopher Goldsmith, CEBS, Sibson.

Behavioral Economics Improve Workforce Health Decisions. Christopher Goldsmith, Sibson Consulting. Society of Human Resource Management (online article; January 3, 2012)
http://www.shrm.org/hrdisciplines/benefits/Articl es/Pages/BehavioralEconomics_Health.aspx

Center for Health Incentives and Behavioral Economics at the Leonard Davis Institute. University of Pennsylvania.
http://chibe.upenn.edu

Role of Culture

The concept of a culture of health within an organization is a popular one. Successful companies often point to the strength of their culture as a significant contributor toward success of their workplace wellness programs and overall health of their organization. In general, culture is the very fabric that employees can learn and experience directly what their company stands for. Culture is often the one thing that differentiates one company from another. For example, if you ever flown on Southwest Airlines, you may understand the unique and quirky culture that their founder, Herb Kelleher, instilled. While other airlines exist, no one can recreate or copy the exact same culture that makes Southwest so special, making customers want to fly again and again.

When it comes to workplace wellness, organizations have had to develop a sub-culture within their existing culture to support health.   By definition, culture is the sum total of social influences on attitudes and behaviors, including shared values, norms, peer support, touch points and climate within an organization (Judd Allen). Taking it a step further, a culture of health takes into account the specific environmental support embedded in a culture.

But why is a culture of health such an important organizational strategy to strive for?
The supporting mechanisms of a business strategy are typically part of a culture. Employees perform or carry out functions in support of a business strategy. Therefore, without employees you don't have business strategy. Or said in another way, without healthy and productive employees, your business strategy cannot be fully achieved. In competitive markets, companies need whatever edge they can get.

Companies who approach and incorporate health and productivity as part of their business strategy experience superior human capital and achieve significantly better financial outcomes

Case in point: Johnson and Johnson, starting in 1978, progressively invested in health and wellness programs setting a goal to have the world's healthiest workforce. They recognized the need for long-term commitment to a culture of health focusing on five key areas:

- Leadership and Commitment
- Enterprise Programs
- Policies and Procedures
- Promotion and Communications
- Measurement and Results

Taking a long-term perspective, they knew that a culture of health is not achieved overnight. Through small, consistent steps they designed and implemented a comprehensive and integrated approach to employee health management. As found in the J & J credo: "The health of the employee is inseparable from the health of the corporation." [14] Granted, it probably helped that J&J was already in the business of health as it was consistent with the line of products they created, but the spirit of this vision and their strategy are scalable to organizations large and small.

J&J's results in the area of health and wellness have been well documented through industry conferences. And compared to industry norms as set forth by CDC, their metrics on health risk factors were below industry norms for unhealthy eating, obesity, inactivity, hypertension, cholesterol, tobacco use and stress. Note how all of these items are related to controllable behaviors.

What does a culture of health look like?

While we can look to leading organizations for best-in-class culture indicators, it's important to understand the common features successful companies all possess:

- Strong leadership advocacy and role models
- Managers and supervisors supporting employees taking time to address health and wellness needs
- Environmental support such as cafeterias with nutritional offerings, physical activity, ergonomics, smoke-free workplaces, policies for work/life balance, time off, sick/leave
- Benefits and Plan Design to support access such was affordability, telemedicine onsite and convenient access and incentives

- Consistent, frequent communications year round. Branding helps.
- Recognizing employees for their achievements, sharing testimonials
- Transparency, visibility to goals, metrics and results
- Reflection of what is important to employees and their families. Supporting their community service activities, engaging in organized wellness events such as walks/runs, charitable events.

It can seem overwhelming for an organization to implement all of these components. However, it's important to take an incremental approach and offer what's meaningful to your organization.

R.C. Bigelow, Inc. based in Fairfield, Connecticut, the makers of Bigelow Tea, support a culture of wellness by offering employees information and tools they need to be successful in improving their overall health and wellness, which will enable them to live longer, happier lives. This long-term vision is taking an employee-first approach. Bigelow demonstrates their support through a healthy awards luncheon recognizing participants who achieved high completion rates on nutrition, weight maintenance and fitness programs. The culture identifies the recognition as a source of inspiration to achieve their goals, as well as a sign of commitment from the organization.

Luncheons, incentives, recognitions and other touch points all weave into the cultural fabric employees come to learn, expect and appreciate. This is what defines a culture.

Wellness Programs
To Implement

Given their widespread availability and exposure, the types of wellness program components you can offer have become common knowledge. Most employers deliver wellness programs directly through their health plans (such as Aetna, Anthem BlueCross Blue Shield, Cigna, and United Healthcare). Specialized wellness vendors and community health resources also provide a valuable portion of wellness services that employers use. There are also a number of wellness programs developed and managed directly by an employer. As a result, there's a good chance that your company is offering several, if not many, of these already. And if not, you don't have to go far to find out what those programs are.

Here's a sample list of many of the typical workplace wellness programs and services offered. You probably can think of a few more:

- Preventive care (e.g., medical, dental, vision checkups)
- Mammograms

- Biometric screenings (such as blood pressure, cholesterol, glucose, body fat)
- Health coaching programs (onsite or telephonic)
- Disease management programs (onsite or telephonic)
- Online health training/education (self-directed)
- Onsite healthy lifestyle programs (e.g., nutrition, weight loss, stress reduction, smoking cessation)
- Health webinars/seminars (live and recorded)
- Wellness challenges (games, steps, weight loss, exercise minutes)
- Health fairs
- Flu shots and immunizations
- Health risk appraisal
- Nurse line or other health decision phone support
- Personal health record
- Environmental support (e.g., tobacco-free campus, healthy vending machines, healthy options in the cafeteria, walking trails)
- HR policies (e.g., flexible work schedules, break policies, PTO policies)

- Ergonomic adaptations and awareness
- Regular communications
- "Cycle to work" program

The goal is not to offer as many programs as possible, but rather offer the right grouping that makes sense for your organization and your strategy. Again, if you think about the Population Health Management approach, you want to offer programs that support the spectrum of health.

While you should tailor your wellness programs to support your organization's strategy and culture, it's important that you continue to focus on offering a variety of programs that support a Population Health Management approach. This will only help to maximize the value of the financial investment and outcomes in the long term.

Planning Wellness Model, Chapman

Program Model	Quality of Work Life Approach	Traditional Approach	Population Health Approach
Main Features	• Fun Activity focus • No Risk reduction • No high risk focus • Not HCM oriented • All voluntary • Site-based only • No personalization • Minimal incentives • No spouses served • No evaluation	• Mostly health focus • Some risk reduction • Little high risk focus • Limited HCM oriented • All voluntary • Site-based only • Weak personalization • Modest incentives • Few spouses served • Weak evaluation	• Add productivity • Strong risk reduction • Strong high risk focus • Strong HCM oriented • Some required activity • Site and virtual • Strongly personal • Major incentives • Many spouses served • Rigorous evaluation
Primary Focus	Morale-Oriented	Activity-Oriented	Results-Oriented

Source: *Chapman, Planning Wellness,* Chapman Institute, 2008, p. 213. (Available on Amazon.com)

What Do the Best Companies Offer

To illustrate the application of wellness programs by award winning and highly recognized companies, you don't have to go far. Rather than reinventing the wheel, I recommend you look at organizations that have provided successful workplace wellness programs. While success can be defined in many different ways, one largely acceptable and valuable way to find such leaders is to look at industry rankings and recognitions. The following presents a list of industry organizations that recognize employers in a formal way for their efforts toward workplace wellness.

The Top 46 Healthiest Companies to Work for in America

The Greatist.com, a leading, trusted source for all things fitness, health and happiness produces an annual Greatest 47 Healthiest Companies to Work for in America. While I can't vouch for the scientific nature of their evaluation process, Greatest.com does claim to rank companies based upon their exemplary health benefits and whether the business offers perks that truly go above and beyond what's expected.

If anything, it's a fun and interesting way to get some ideas and benchmark how employers are approaching workplace wellness.

Here are a few companies that made the Top 46 Healthiest Companies list in 2013. To see the entire list, go to their website:

http://greatist.com/health/healthiest-companies

General Electric (GE)

GE tackles the global health problem with their HealthyImagination campaign, designed to increase quality, access and affordability of health care. GE employees live and breathe their mission with great health benefits, maternity and paternity leave, onsite gyms at most locations, and HealthAhead — a wellness site with resources and tools to get and stay healthy. They're also encouraged to commit to making a small, health-related choice (such as standing more) every day through the company's "Small Changes" program.

Google

Google employees have a lot to smile about. Boasting an in-office slide, Ping-Pong tables and scooters to make it to meetings on time, Google HQ considers play a top priority. The super popular tech company makes healthy eating a cinch with visible nutrition labels and a cafeteria designed with behavioral economics in mind, putting healthier choices at the forefront and keeping portion sizes in check. Though Google admits its employees had a serious M&M addiction, the company took action by storing the candy in opaque containers and displaying healthier snacks, such as pistachios, in glass jars. And for any and all aches and pains, Google's got an onsite physical therapist and chiropractor.

Mayo Clinic

Because teamwork makes the dream work, Mayo Clinic celebrates achievements with recognition funds for employee milestones and group efforts. To keep those noggins sharp, the company offers instructor-led and online classes for professional growth and education. Mayo Clinic's LiveWell program helps employees find tools and resources to make healthy choices, and if you've got a question, the "Ask Mayo Clinic 24/7" medical resource line has got the answer. The company also boasts a Healthy Living Center, the goal of which is to provide an inclusive wellness program for all employees. Achieving work-life balance at Mayo Clinic is trouble-free with flexible hours, maternity and paternity leave, and funeral leave.

Hasbro

We all grew up wanting to work for a toy company, but this is one childhood dream job that holds up to scrutiny (sorry, professional ninjas). With nearly 6,000 employees working toward making children happy, Hasbro was recently named one of Fortune's 100 Best Companies to Work For in the U.S. — but it's also one of the healthiest. Not only does their Rhode Island headquarters supply access to a weekly healthy veggie subscription box, but twice a month they put on a "wellness workshop" that teaches employees about the value of a diverse range of topics such as mindfulness, yoga, and massage. They also host fitness-centered events such as the Hasbro 5k. Add that to their on-site gyms that offer classes in Zumba, Pilates, yoga kickboxing and even hula hooping, and Hasbro is clearly a company that's dedicated to keeping their employees happy and healthy for as long as possible.

Angie's List

Repeatedly ranked as one of the best places to work in Indiana by the state's Chamber of Commerce, Angie's List is also one of the healthiest. With a full-time Wellness Director and personal trainer on staff, the company is all about giving incentives for healthy habits. Employees earn time off for running a marathon, $1,000 to quit smoking, and up to $300 in gift cards for taking part in the company's 30 different wellness programs. The programs cover topics like stress management and healthy eating, and offer heart health assessments, flu shots and CPR classes. Most impressive is their "Garden Club," a program that helps each and every employee learn how to grow and maintain their own vegetable patch on site.

Fowler White Boggs

Law isn't always seen as the healthiest profession, but Fowler White Boggs is bucking that trend with some of the best employee benefits in the country. In addition to attending one-on-one coaching with registered dieticians and nurses, Fowler White Boggs employees can also earn healthcare discounts for meeting certain biometric stats (like lowered blood pressure and BMI). And their lunch breaks are hands-down the coolest: the company offers a "Lunch 'n' Learn" lecture series during which employees can learn about health and wellness topics while savoring healthy meals. The firm is also tops at encouraging pro bono work to get employee's legal expertise to those in need.

Business Council of Fairfield County (Connecticut) Healthy Employer Recognitions

The Healthy Workplace Employer Recognition program is an initiative of The Business Council of Fairfield County's Wellness Roundtable. The program showcases some of the best practices and breakthrough thinking for effective promotion of employee health and wellness of employers in and around the Fairfield County, Connecticut area.

Pitney Bowes

Pitney Bowes has worked to build a Culture of Health since 1993. From the top levels of the organization, investment in the health of employees has proven important for the overall success of the corporation, providing value for its employees and shareholders. The overall goal is to have healthy, productive, engaged employees. Their programs focus on modifiable health behaviors, improving consumerism, helping employees use their health plan wisely and having a healthy work environment.

They believe that employees who take action to manage their health are happier, more engaged and more productive than those who do not. Employees also save money on health care, both for themselves and for the company. For all these reasons, employees are encouraged to take charge of their health through such simple steps as eating well, exercising, taking advantage of preventive care screenings and working with care providers to manage health conditions that require it.

R.C. Bigelow

The mission of the R.C. Bigelow program is to create a culture of wellness by giving the employees the information and tools they need to be successful in improving their overall health and wellness as well as encourage them to use the resources of its health insurance provider and community services. They strive to provide a supportive environment of work/life balance and a place where employees can come to find answers on health and wellness related questions. They seek to continuously educate employees through their "Be HealthTea" wellness program with lunch and learns on various health issues, annual wellness fairs and monthly wellness postings to name a few. The Wellness Team and Wellness Champions are constantly seeking new ways to bring the message of wellness to employees in all of R.C. Bigelow's locations.

Daymon Worldwide

At Daymon Worldwide, associates come first. This basic principle of the culture carries over to all that is done including health and wellness programs. Daymon's corporate wellness program is focused on providing the right access, tools and support to help manage and maintain the health of associates and their family members. Each year, the company's goal is to increase preventive care participation, improve health status and enhance the lives of all of its associates by helping them get healthy.   Daymon engages employees in a fun way through several Gamification wellness programs (Shape Up and Passport to Health) which are well-received by employees.

To learn more about the Healthy Employer Recognitions program offered by the Business Council of Fairfield County, go to http://www.businessfairfield.com/healthy-workplace-best-practices-award-recognition-program/.

National Business Group on Health

If you want to know what nationally recognized employers are doing for their health and wellness programs, study the winners of the coveted BEST EMPLOYERS FOR HEALTHY LIFESTYLES® award program. The National Business Group on Health acknowledges and rewards member companies for demonstrating creative, comprehensive and effective solutions that improve employee health, productivity and well-being.

The Best Employers for Healthy Lifestyles® award recognize the most outstanding workplace well-being programs — programs that are comprehensive, achieve strong levels of engagement and improve health outcomes. The Best Employers for Healthy Lifestyles® awards program, which started in 2004, serves as a means of sharing successful interventions, strategies and services, and illustrates best practices that can be emulated by other companies. The focus and specific criteria for the award are updated annually with evidence-based standards that reflect the evolving field of workplace well-being and health promotion.

There's also a Global Distinction for The Best Employers for Healthy Lifestyles® award that recognizes companies that are dedicated to impacting the physical, psychological and emotional health, well-being and productivity of global employees and their dependents. This award acknowledges strategy and action taken at the level of both corporation and country. The intent is to reward those companies that are leveraging a wide variety of tactics (e.g., covered benefits, health communications, health promotion, etc.) to truly change the health profile of their extended worldwide workforce.

Sixty five employers were recognized in 2013 at the Business Group's Institute on Innovation in Workforce Well-being Leadership Summit held in Washington, DC. To learn more, go to their website at http://www.businessgrouphealth.org/benchmarking/awards.cfm.

Well Workplace Awards - WELCOA

The cornerstone of the Wellness Council of America is the "Well Workplace" Awards process. Their innovative initiative recognizes quality and excellence in worksite health promotion. Driven by a pre-defined set of worksite wellness criteria, organizations of all kinds compete to be recognized as one of America's Healthiest Companies. On the Wellness Council's website, you can review case studies that detail the process and outcomes of Well Workplace Award winning companies. Members of WELCOA can access numerous other case studies as part of their membership. Go to www.welcoa.org for more information.

Communications

Why Communications are so Important

According to the U.S. Bureau of Labor Statistics, benefits account for 30 percent or more of employee total compensation. A considerable amount of time and effort goes into planning and implementing benefits programs for employees. On the contrary, to promote those benefits, over two-thirds of companies[2] spend less than $25,000 on benefit communication, with the vast majority of spend exclusively on print and postage costs. This would equate to 0.25 percent or less if your total benefit plan costs were $10M.

In comparison, companies who need consumers to buy their products often budget between 2 percent to 5 percent (and even more) of sales for marketing and advertising programs which are essentially communications efforts aimed at engaging people. While the difference in marketing budgets can vary by industry, companies understand that it's not easy to influence behavior change and to sustain it; how do you attract and retain loyal customers effectively without breaking the bank? Benefits and workplace wellness programs are no different; companies have an obligation to invest the time and effort to find ways to effectively communicate benefits to their employees.

Overall, we're not doing a good enough job communicating benefits. Budgeting matters aside, less than 40 percent of employers think their benefit communications are effective. Employees also believe benefit communications are less effective (about 33 percent).[2]

One of the more significant benefit communication challenges that companies face is getting employees and their families engaged year round in wellness programs. While companies may follow the traditional tactic of communicating during the annual benefits open enrollment period or when there's a big event, 78 percent of companies find it difficult to continually inform month after month about benefits. For those who do communicate regularly, the majority relies on a "one size fits all" approach rather than a personalized one.

Why do most companies fail at communicating benefits?

- Lack of a sufficient budget
- Inadequate staff to manage
- A communications skills gap

While everyone would love to have more of a budget and increased staff, the new norm is for organizations to run lean and mean; do more with less. However, to gain a competitive edge, employers are tasking employees to expand their skills base. Through this process, many organizations are learning about a skills gap that is impacting productivity in the United States, and which is not just about technical skills.

Adecco Group North America's conducted a survey of senior executives (VP and above) in 2013 gathering insights into the current state of the economy and employment situation. Overwhelming, a majority of senior executives (92 percent) feel that there is a gap in the U.S. workforce skills. Surprisingly, the majority of the gap is not technical (22 percent), leadership (14 percent) or computer skills (12 percent) that the U.S. workforce is lacking today. Senior executives feel the gap is in the soft skills (44 percent) such as communication, critical thinking, creativity and collaboration. Therefore, workplace wellness professionals who can enhance their own soft skills, including communications, will have an edge in creating more successful workplace wellness programs.

Sustaining your communications throughout the year can go a long way toward keeping benefits and wellness top of mind. Companies who can communicate effectively throughout the year on a regular basis have higher success in engaging employees, building awareness and influencing desired changes.

Benefits Communications Frequency	% of Companies
Few times a year	34%
Year round, hardly a month without communication	29%
Only when there's a big event (e.g. enrollment, change)	27%
Most of the year	10%

Source: *Inside Benefits Communications 2012*, Benz Communications

Another vital, but overlooked factor by companies in communications is diversity. Whether it's cultural, cross-generational, gender, financial, educational level or geographical differences, diversity contributes to the complexity of communicating your message. Ideally, to increase their effectiveness, communications should tailor to a specific audience and be crafted to enlist a unique action. Otherwise, the message may go unread or not understood if the audience doesn't get it.

Remember, it's not always what you say, but how and when you say it. Communications methods and styles need to be a "best fit" to your organization's culture, and incorporate an equally balanced mixed of frequency, method and context to be effective.

Cast a Wide Net When Communicating

In a perfect world, companies would employ a wide array of communication tactics frequently and often tailored to a diverse group of people. But we know that's not always realistic. What methods do you rely upon? Which ones are most effective?

- One to one in-person meetings
- One to many / group setting
- Paper distributed to employees at work or home
- E-mails
- Texting
- Intranet or Internet
- Live Online Meetings and Webinars
- Video or podcasts (YouTube)
- Blogs (WordPress)

- Social networks (Facebook or Twitter)
- Diversity and wellness committees
- Wellness champions

Nearly two-thirds of companies use a "one size fits all" method for communicating benefits at work[2]. The challenge is that the war for people's attention is competitive. At work, employees need to focus on their jobs, manage others, perform company required trainings and participate in numerous meetings. There is a continual drive to prioritize. How can you be strategic to get your message out? Most people are also overwhelmed by the volume and frequency of bombarding messages received through e-mails, text, television, radio, U.S. mail and billboards, whether consciously or unconsciously. We never know for sure which tactics will work and get our message through. Additionally, most companies don't have the resources, skill set or time to create top flight communications.

But one fact should be kept in mind, 84 percent of companies who do effectively communicate year round are more successful and achieve their (benefit/wellness) goals. [2]

Shortly after I started managing benefits for a mid-sized company, I evaluated the utilization of its Employee Assistance Plan (EAP). I discovered an extremely low rate of members using the plan. The EAP's account representative had also shared how the company was on the lower end of the spectrum compared to most of their customers in terms of member utilization.

Through collaboration with the EAP, our benefits consultant and internal company resources, we devised a simple plan to communicate over the next six months about a different feature of the EAP at which point we would measure the utilization again. Since we didn't have a budget, we had to be creative in our approach. We used a number of tactics including:

- Distributed the generic flyers created by the EAP through e-mail to all employees.
- Included an EAP flyer with new hire communications. (This included posting of several key resources from the EAP on the company's intranet.)
- Inserted an EAP flyer in the Family Medical Leave/Disability package sent to employees going out on disability. (This was a great opportunity to promote how EAP services could help in a variety of ways.)

- Promoted EAP during Benefits Open Enrollment
- Pushed out several targeted communications throughout the year about how the EAP provided services to support several tragic and key events that occurred that year

As a result of these efforts, participation rates increased dramatically. According to the vendor, the company ranked in the top quartile of utilization for all their customers the following year.

Over time, we continued to enhance communication efforts in a number of other cross-selling methods. The organization recently implemented Yammer, a social media tool like Facebook used for internal communication purposes. Messages from the EAP and other benefit plan providers that impact the whole organization are posted timely on Yammer and shared with a large group of people quickly and effectively.

Sometimes a simple change, like raising awareness, can make a difference.

How to Develop a Communications Strategy

To get started, it's important to write down what your communications needs are. Documenting what the goals are not only helps to keep you accountable, it also helps to develop a foundation for your communications strategy. Sounds simple enough, but only 22 percent of companies actually document their communications strategy[2]. Companies with written communications strategies that link benefit communications tactics with overall benefit programs, as well as with business goals, are more successful.

Documenting your strategy will enhance your benefit communications effectiveness as it will accomplish a number of things:

- Force you to be specific about what your goals are
- Identify your game plan for how you will deliver communications
- Allow you to measure your effectiveness
- Evaluate and improve upon communications tactics year over year

- Sustain a proactive mode whereby you control how and when to execute with a purpose

While writing a communications strategy can take different forms, there are a number of basic and widely used steps that can help you get started. I discovered a practical and effective method to develop a communications strategy from Benz Communications' *Inside Benefits Communications Report 2012* that recommends a Six Step process:

1. Define the problem and identify top goals; how will you measure
2. What are the key traits of your audience and behaviors that will help meet your goals
3. Create a detailed communications plan including key messages, tactics and timing
4. Implement the plan using various methods
5. Measure your outcomes, behaviors; evaluate your success
6. Refine

Using a process like this six step one I outlined will help you clarify your purpose and produce a plan to address it head on. Documenting it out can also help gain support from leaders who may need to approve your actions and possible budgetary needs.

Content to Communicate

Where do you find information to promote workplace wellness programs? This is often a challenge for many HR professionals.

You may not have the luxury of an in-house communications team at your disposal that can create all of your wellness communications. You may not have the time, capacity or the budget to develop your own communications.   To be effective and efficient, you need to tap into what's readily available and available at no cost

Health Plans

A primary source of information should be your health plans. Aetna, Cigna, UnitedHealth and Blue Cross Blue Shield plans and many other health plans deliver pre-made flyers, posters, e-mails and even brief videos on various health topics to promote the health and wellness programs that they deliver for your organization. Ask your account representative for access to an online toolkit or directory of such resources.

I've had the opportunity to work with Aetna for long period of time implementing and managing health and wellness programs. I've tapped into their communication kits available through the Employer section of Aetna.com. While an employer needs to be an Aetna customer to access these kits since it requires a username and password, this resource can be invaluable because the Communication Kit includes PDF flyers, pre-designed e-mail messaging, posters and even brief video messages describing what each program is and how to tap into them.

Your Employee Assistance Program (EAP) is another practical and inexpensive method to locate communications materials for your wellness program. EAP's provides a wealth of online resources including articles, for example, on a wide spectrum of health topics. With their permission, you can publish articles on a regular basis on your organizations intranet, news blog or through distribution by e-mail. Each month, you can complement your communications efforts using EAP sources.

Through my professional experience, I've worked with Ceridian who provided Lifeworks EAP. As part of their program offering, they offer training credits which can be applied toward live webinars hosted by Ceridian health professionals. From their training offerings, I was able to identify a number of health related webinars that yielded a number of ways to support workplace wellness.

- First, I created a "Healthy Webinar" series that lasted six months. Once each month, I offered a different live seminar on a health topic presented by a professional expert who worked for Ceridian. For one hour, each expert led an interactive presentation on topics addressing relevant topics such as healthy eating, stress reduction and preventive care. The topics were selected because they were important to my organization and consistent with our wellness strategy. I scheduled the events at the beginning of the calendar year, and then communicated in advance all of the sessions with instructions on how to participate. I would also send a reminder communication several weeks in advance to drum up participation.

- Ceridian would also send out a PDF of the presentation to all those who registered. I would also post the presentation on our company's internal website for viewing at any time by any associate. Since the presentation was live, the time wasn't always convenient for associates. Shortly after the presentation was held, a brief communication would be sent out to inform everyone about the materials.

- Next, I created a brief news article summarizing the main points from the presentation which was published on the company's intranet news portal. This helped to promote the program globally to the organization.

- Lastly, I encouraged participation in the health webinars as a way to earn "points" toward a completely separate wellness challenge whereby employees earned points for participating in a wide range of health and wellness programs offered by the company. We called it Passport to Health. This cross-marking approach served as a great vehicle to engage associates in a wider range of wellness programs offered by the company.

Decentralized organizations are challenged in communicating effectively and timely because employees are located in multiple locations. Delivering wellness programs in a cost-effective manner is difficult. Organizations with a captive audience in one or several locations, however, can design and implement wellness programs more efficiently.

Industry Sources for Communications Materials

WELCOA (Wellness Council of America) provides a wealth of free resources on their website (www.welcoa.org) including a library of pre-designed PowerPoint presentations on health and wellness topics. As a member of WELCOA, you can access an even larger number of presentations than what's available for free. This is an excellent way to deliver quality wellness information on a consistent and professional basis.

Next, you can tap into a deep source of information available through industry associations, government agencies and non-profit organizations. Most maintain resources online through their website. As long as you make adequate reference to the source or get their permission, you can use a lot of pre-made, ready–to-use communication pieces.

Take the month of February as an example, also known as "heart month." A National Awareness Campaign for Women centering on Heart Disease is National Wear Red Day held on February 7, 2014. The website www.hearttruth.gov is a great online resource for information to help you promote women's heart health. Many organizations often carry the theme of heart health throughout the month, capitalizing on the heart theme started on Valentine's Day. Therefore, you can get great mileage early in the year on heart health.

One simple way to locate these industry resources is by using a wellness observance calendar. A number of businesses create a month-by-month wellness observance calendar that lists out health observances along with the organization promoting it. Just "google" or do an internet search on the term Wellness Observance Calendar. You'll be amazed at the number of valuable results you will get.

Each year, Aetna creates an annual wellness observances calendar for their customers which include links to communications resources to support all of the Aetna wellness programs. Many of those resources are unique to Aetna and their programs. However, other health plans provide similar tools and communication pieces to help promote the wellness programs they offer.

Another great wellness calendar that I like to download is from the National Wellness Institute (NWI). Besides providing dozens of causes throughout the calendar year, the events that the NWI promote are exclusively geared toward health and wellness topics. The NWI calendar provides links to non-profit health organizations that are well-known and often supported by an employee population.

A few years ago, when I was tasked with delivering a communications effort on diabetes awareness, I found a great resource to support diabetes awareness. My organization had implemented a medical plan enhancement to cover nutritional counseling, diabetic supplies and glucose monitors at 100 percent with no member out-of-pocket for those with diabetes. At the time, Bret Michaels from the rock band Poison had become a prominent spokesperson for Diabetes.Org. Their website included a link to a free risk survey to help understand your risk for diabetes. The survey was an easy and fun way to introduce the concept of diabetes awareness that was supported by an independent, well-respected organization. You can find similar resources for most other health causes.

Choosing Wisely
The National Business Coalition on Health, along with the generous support of Pacific Business Group on Health, partnered with Consumer Reports to create The *Choosing Wisely* Employer Toolkit for employers to use to educate their employees about the dangers and issues associated with the overuse of health care services.

These materials can help you launch the *Choosing Wisely* campaign with your employees or integrate it with your current communication efforts, all with your own brand. These materials are intended for broad distribution. They're written to "speak" to diverse workforces across a variety of industries.

http://www.nbch.org/Choosing-Wisely-Employer-Toolkit

Centers for Disease Control (CDC) started the National Healthy Worksite Program to assist employers in implementing science and practice-based prevention and wellness strategies that will lead to specific, measureable health outcomes to reduce chronic disease rates. For most employers, chronic diseases — such as heart disease, stroke, cancer, obesity, arthritis and diabetes — are among the most prevalent, costly and preventable of all health problems. The National Healthy Worksite Program seeks to promote good health through prevention, reduce chronic illness and disability, and improve productivity outcomes that contribute to employers' competitiveness.

The website offers a wide range of resources, training, case studies and toolkits that provide ready-made communication pieces to help promote workplace wellness programs.

http://www.cdc.gov/nationalhealthyworksite/index.html

There are a wide range of great resources to tap into for communications support. It just takes a little time and effort to find them.

Influence of Social Media and Social Networking on Wellness

Social media (as defined in Wikipedia) refers to interaction among people in which they create, share, and/or exchange information and ideas in virtual communities and networks (using technology). However, when you and I think about social media or social networking, what comes to mind? Facebook, Twitter, LinkedIn, YouTube, and a host of other online or mobile device applications used on our i-Phone, Android, i-Pad or tablet.

It's so common now for people to get their information about news, current events and products through social media. People are virtually living their lives online. Social media is the number one activity that people do on the web. At the time that I'm writing this, a new movie was released about a man who had a relationship with the voice on his i-Phone which totally optimizes the level of engagement people have with their technology.

By 2015, more individuals will access the internet via mobile devices than through PCs or other wired devices according to International Data Corporation. And on these mobile devices they will be using a host of online and mobile apps to access information and connect with people. As benefit and wellness professionals, we need to embrace this fact as it's an opportunity to engage employees.

Nevertheless, given this recent trend, it's astonishing that 72 percent of employers are *not* communicating through any type of mobile device. In his groundbreaking book, Socialnomics, Erik Qualman indicated that 70 percent of big company CEO's (as of July 2012) have no presence on social networks. If CEOs aren't going to lead organizations through this new paradigm shift, who will?

To get an unusually insightful and entertaining appreciation of how social media is transforming our lives, I recommend you watch Social Media Video 2013, a brief video that puts social media and social networking revolution into perspective. You can find the video on YouTube, and also on the Socialnomics website. As a result of watching the video the question you'll ask isn't whether you *should* use social media, it's *how well* you plan to use it.

Social media and web-based tools for health care and wellness are expected to grow. More and more technology companies are emerging to take advantage of the opportunity to reach so many people in a convenient way. One of the significant reasons why social networking within health care is seen as a growth area is because of the influence of friends on our health.

Gamification
Did you know that the average person today accumulates at least 10,000 hours of gaming by age 21? The time your son or daughter (or you) are spending on XBOX, Playstation or Wii counts toward this total. That's about two hours each and every day if they started from age eight.

Millennial's and Generation Y's who enter the workforce are comfortable toward learning through use of technology, and more specifically online games, almost as if they are programmed to do so. Today, the average age of a game player is 35. [3] Gaming is not just for kids.

As a result, Gamification has emerged as the new way to engage and motivate employees. Essentially, Gamification is the use of game techniques in a non-game situation to help motivate people and drive behavior. Participants follow different scenarios and rules tracking their progress through various levels earning points and other recognitions for their accomplishments in a competitive manner, either on a team or individual basis over time.

Gartner predicts that by year 2015, 70 percent of Global 2000 companies will use one form of Gamification solutions. [15]

We're all familiar with the cultural shift toward lifestyle wellness mainly because it's visible. However, there's also a shift toward self-directed and informal learning. Gamification and related online wellness programs are a great "communications" vehicle for employees that are self-directed and informal. However, the main reason why Gamification is becoming so popular is because of its effectiveness.

According to training experts, most new learning occurs informally. Online games are a great way to engage employees in a "less than formal" corporate manner.

Keep in mind, nearly 35 percent of today's workforce in the United States is comprised of Generation Y, and by 2020 they will represent 46 percent of the workforce. Therefore, it's predicted that a larger segment of the workforce will be more aligned with online gaming.

Through my own experience managing wellness challenges, I've seen the positive effects of Gamification on wellness and behavior change. Using the Get Active tool, powered by ShapeUp, teams of employees compete for the most exercise minutes, most steps walked and the highest percentage weight lost. At the end of eight weeks, the team of employees who scored the best in one of the three categories is recognized for their accomplishments. One of the main drivers behind online gaming programs like ShapeUp is the effect of a social support system on health outcomes. People do better when they feel connected to a social support network encouraging them to reach specific and shared goals.

While financial rewards, prizes and recognitions often fuel participation, the biggest "win" companies can gain from such wellness challenges is the behavior change people make that they normally would not have made on their own. There is an inherent social aspect adopted and embraced by all generations which helps to make using the tool fun. Participants are motivated by the immediate accountability to others on their team. While you can attempt to estimate an ROI, the most significant outcome from these types of wellness challenges are the anecdotal stories shared by participants. Prevalent themes include how employees lost weight, exercised more and started eating better as a result of the program. Often they didn't want to let their teammates down. Accountability to others is one of the main driving forces behind the success of Gamification and online health communities.

Here's a list of online Gamification companies you may want to consider:

Gamification Companies	
Keas	ShapeUp
Get The World Moving	Mindbloom
Fooducate	Nexercise
Daily Challenge	Bunchball
RunKeeper	Azumio
Whaoo Fitness	Achievement
Badgville	BlueOcean Brain
YouMeHealth	Rypple
FitNow	Weight Watchers International
MyFitness Pal	Health Enhancement Systems

The Value of Branding Your Wellness Program

When it comes to communicating benefits, it's recommended to keep things simple. It's overwhelming and confusing as it is for an employee to understand what benefits their company offers them, let alone how best to use each program to their advantage. But what can you do to enhance the recognition of your wellness programs and take action? One tactic is branding.

Organizations who can brand their wellness programs simplify the recognition process and increase the engagement in wellness programs. For example, rather than communicate ten different health and wellness programs (each uniquely distinct), it's simpler and more strategic to let employees know about a "Healthy Living" wellness program that is designed to help them achieve health and balance in their life.

Creating a high level vision or proposition about what your health/wellness program is all about can help connect with employees more on an emotional or cognitive level that is meaningful to them, which may be a trigger of intrinsic motivation.

Branding is used heavily in business world to promote the products and services of a company. The branding process may not necessarily promote the specific product or service, however, the company is essentially communicating a message about what they believe in: integrity, trust, fun. The person would then connect or associate with those concepts and hopefully be more likely to try their products.

Branding your wellness program accomplishes several objectives:

- Reflects an organization's commitment to a culture of health
- Provides consistent messaging on programs that employees can trust
- Enables enhanced recognition by employees to know what you're communicating relates back to your wellness programs
- Develop good will / equity in your wellness programs overtime (assuming you've done a good job managing the other programs). When you roll out a new program and link to your wellness brand, you can gain greater awareness and adoption

Create Your Plan Early, Then Execute Methodically

Developing your communications plan early will help you succeed on a variety of levels.

First, the process will help you identify what your informational or content needs will be. For example, increasing participation in the health risk appraisals may be a top goal for the upcoming year. As a result, you'll need to locate resources to support your communications efforts around health risk appraisals. Can your health plan or wellness vendor provide communication pieces that you can mail, e-mail, publish online, etc....to your general population?

Are you offering financial incentives for completing an annual preventive exam? Distribute a flyer or message along with paystubs or announce in periodic meetings. Get this on the agenda of any upcoming meetings where a large audience may be and promote, promote, promote!

Secondly, developing a communications plan early will help to create realistic timelines. Do you have other wellness programs or company initiatives being rolled out about the same time you want to communicate information about your special wellness program? This may cause confusion and cause employees to ignore one or several of your messages.   Be mindful of timing.

Developing a communications plan in advance can help you coordinate with other key resources within your organization that can support your communication efforts. You may have HR leads and business leaders throughout the organization who are willing and able to promote your programs during team meetings or other events they are holding.   While you may be developing your plans from a corporate office, local offices may have local culture and communication needs that are different than other group within your company.

Additionally, creating a timeline of when you want to communicate different wellness programs creates visibility for others on your team or those within your vendor partners. Sharing your timeline in advance can allow your "virtual team" to research and provide valuable content that you need. If you plan a direct mail piece, you inevitably have to plan well in advance (at least three to four weeks) to meet print fulfillment requirements. Give yourself time to research and select a dependent print fulfillment vendor who can meet your needs.

Inclusion is the Key: 1 + 1 = 3
Share your wellness goals and objectives with each
of your benefit plan vendors. Include your benefit
plan contacts as a "committee" who can support
and provide direction. They often are working with
other employers and organizations on wellness
initiatives. As a result, they can share lessons
learned, challenges to address and potentially
leverage work that's already been done for your
particular programs.   Including your vendors can
not only develop your relationship, but may be able
to make connections to solutions that they normally
would not be aware of, even if your vendor is
remotely involved in wellness activities such as a
life insurance or disability carrier),

Charting the Communications Course
Mentioned earlier, most organizations don't
document their communications strategy.
Documenting doesn't have to mean creating a 50-
page charter with footnotes and addendums.   You
can create a simple one-page summary that outlines
your both your overall strategy and tactical
approach.

I like to create an Excel chart where the first column represents each of the communication methods I can use. Then, each of the subsequent columns can represent a different month of the calendar. You can liken it to a project plan. To help manage your efforts, include special events that are scheduled such as health fairs or biometric screenings.

Whatever method you choose to track your communications, it's important to document your plan and then share it with others on your team, your vendor partners and anyone else who may be able to contribute and help take ownership.

Metrics and Evaluation

Measuring Workplace Wellness Effectiveness

What you don't measure, you can't manage.
This management adage often referenced back to
Peter Drucker, hailed by *BusinessWeek* as "the man
who invented management", can be conveyed and
interpreted in many different ways. If you don't
measure something, how do you know if it's getting
better or worse? Just like people need to measure
and monitor their own health metrics like blood
pressure, cholesterol and weight in order to make
adjustments to their lifestyle, workplace wellness
programs need to be measured in a variety of ways
to help enhance their effectiveness and
meaningfulness for the organization (people) they
support.

Organizations measure workplace wellness on a number of levels an in a variety of ways:

- Participation levels
- Behavior change
- Economic returns and investment (ROI)
- Productivity
- Employee satisfaction and engagement
- Benchmark against industry trends
- Submit as a case study to industry journals
- Support application for formal recognitions

At the core, workplace wellness metrics should be telling you a story about whether you're moving toward the goals and objectives set forth.   Tracking metrics will also help to demonstrate the value of your programs and support the efforts outlined in the strategy and planning stages of the Cycle of Wellness.

How can you determine if your programs are working?

If you're just starting out implementing workplace wellness programs, it's probably best you start off with simple, limited but meaningful measurements. Defining the goals of your program and what you hope to accomplish will get you headed in the right direction. Benefits consulting group Willis reported in their HR Focus 2012 a number of easy, low-cost ways to measure and evaluate the effectiveness of your wellness programs.

Determine Baselines for Key Metrics

To track progress on wellness programs, you need a starting point. What are the current levels of participation, health outcomes and health risks of your wellness programs? If you offered a health risk appraisal (HRA) last year, what was the participation rate? Typically, this is reported by the health plan or vendor who manages the appraisal. I recommend that you include measurements for each of the relevant populations who can participate. For example, count the rate of spouses or significant others who are eligible for HRAs as this is an important sub-group to impact.

Set Specific, Measureable and Realistic Goals

If your current reporting reflects a 10 percent participation rate in adult preventive exams in your baseline year, what would be realistic goal in years two and three? Your projection will most likely depend on a number of factors, many of which you have directly influence on such as the programs used to motivate and engage adults. Will you incentivize financially for participation? Do you plan to do targeted and frequent communications on preventive exams?

Perhaps setting a target of 25 percent by year three is realistic given your population group's ability to change. I recommend you benchmark industry norms on what the ideal goals are for your specific wellness programs as this will help manage your expectations. Your health plan should be able to provide this type of benchmarking data.

Track Participation in ALL Wellness Events

If you're offering five different programs, measure all five. You want to at least get a baseline on all five programs. You'll never know which one will be a surprise. I recommend you develop a Wellness Scorecard which can serve as a high-level summary of the most important demographic and wellness program metrics you need to track. Keep it to one page to start.

Willis also recommends performing pre- and post-surveys and asking for testimonials. While these seem like good ideas, you may not always have the luxury or administrative capability to perform them. If a third party manages your wellness programs, they have may have flexibility and process to collect this information. One of the challenges of engaging directly with people about their opinion on a wellness program is compliance. You need to make sure you're following HIPAA and confidentiality laws. If in doubt, it's best to leave it to the experts or to your vendor to manage as they are most likely HIPAA compliant.

Create a Scorecard to Measure Your Program

In the 2011 movie Moneyball, Brad Pitt plays Billy Beane, the general manager of the Oakland Athletics baseball team who works with an assistant general manager Peter Brand, played by Jonah Hill, to assemble a more competitive baseball team. Brand is a young Yale economics graduate with radical ideas on how to assess a player's value. At the core of their strategy is a sophisticated Sabermetric, or empirical analysis of baseball, that incorporates primarily baseball statistics that measures in-game activity.

In the movie, they used this metric approach to scout and analyze players to determine who would potentially be the most productive players for their team. While I don't want to spoil the film, the A's won a record-breaking 20 consecutive games in the first season they start to use their new system.

In 2004, two years after adopting the Sabermetric model, the Boston Red Sox won their first World Series since 1918. As a long-time New York Yankee fan, this is one statistic I still have a hard time accepting.

Today, statistics about workplace wellness programs are everywhere. How does your company stack up against others? Which are the most effective programs? What is your ROI? These statistics have to start someplace. Statistics as reported by surveys and benchmarking reports from consulting firms like Towers Watson, Mercer and Buck Consultants come directly from employers who self-report wellness program activity.

Organizations need to systematically collect and measure the activity on their programs, not just to respond to benchmarking studies, but to know how their programs are doing. While many large organizations use "data warehouses" to manage their health plan data and produce reports with a click of a button, most companies don't have the luxury to have their data compiled so readily.

But the good news is you don't have to have to do data warehousing to measure program activity and make insightful decisions.

One simple and easy way to track and measure your programs is through the use of a wellness scorecard. Growing up, I used to keep score at baseball games. I loved using a Scoremaster scorebook to track who was up at bat and record the game actions like a single, a fly out, a stolen base and how many runs were scored. At the end of the game, you could compile meaningful statistics. Today, fantasy sports players readily mine data on their favorite sports players to identify who has the best on-base percentage, most walks, least number of strike outs and other seemingly obscure facts.

You can develop a simple and meaningful scorebook of your own to track and measure the progress of wellness programs.

There is a long list of health and wellness programs and activities that can be tracked. The secret is to track only those that are relevant to your organization's objectives. In a later chapter of this book, "What Kind of Wellness Programs to Implement," I list over twenty different programs an organization can offer to support workplace wellness. Each of these programs should be measured for what they are expected to do.

For example, you may want to answer the following questions:

- What are the overall participation rates?

- Do you see any improvements in health scores or biometric screenings?

- What was the response rate to a communications effort?

- Are we making improvements in our population health management strategy?

Presentation and design of your wellness scorecard data is important. You want to design a concise overview of all the top metrics or data points that are easily readable in a quick-glance or snapshot view. The illustration on the next page is an example of a Wellness Dashboard that tracked data since 2010. The company incorporated data already tracked by their health plan through several other, readily available resources such as the health risk appraisal and other standard periodic reporting on Wellness Program participation from various vendors. As you can see, no health data or HIPAA-protected information is shared.

Wellness Dashboard (as of Q2)

Wellness Program Participation	2010	2011	2012	2013
Unique HRA Completions	368	218	250	67
Online Wellness Program Completions	26	30	164	30
MetS Screenings	N/A	486	623	750
Beginning Right Maternity	19	11	25	18
IHL (calls)	30	11	13	5
PHR-Unique Users	241	440	453	330
Disease Management (Nurse Engagement Level) Targeted	N/A	N/A	89	77
Engaged	N/A	N/A	46	36

Healthy Lifestyle Coaching	2010	2011	2012	2013(Q1)
HLC Eligible	1836	1775	1771	1749
HRA Identified	126	214	129	63
Engaged	36	20	51	22

Metabolic Syndrome Results (% out of Range)	2010	2011	2012	2013
Blood Pressure	N/A	56%	53%	
Triglycerides	N/A	20%	17%	
Total Cholesterol	N/A	29%	28%	
HDL	N/A	21%	19%	
LDL	N/A	17%	19%	
Glucose	N/A	16%	16%	
Waist Circum.	N/A	26%	21%	

HRA: Biometric Risk Factors (Reported Lab Values) % at Risk	2010	2011	2012	2013
Prehypertension or hypertension (lab value)	24%	26%	32%	31%
High cholesterol (lab value)	15%	14%	15%	15%
High triglyceride level (lab value)	6%	6%	8%	1%
High blood sugar (lab value)	4%	2%	8%	6%

HRA: Top 5 Self Reported Conditions (% at Risk)	2010	2011	2012	2013
Allergies	29%	31%	26%	28%
High cholesterol	16%	18%	15%	15%
High blood pressure	15%	16%	20%	21%
Lower back problems	14%		14%	15%
Obesity				13%
Headaches	13%	14%		
Asthma		11%		
Depression			13%	

Not in Top 5 for year

HRA Top 5 Modifiable Risk Factors (% at Risk)	2010	2011	2012	2013
Low fruit/vegetables in diet	89%	86%	87%	93%
Inadequate sun protection	66%	62%	63%	73%
Inadequate exercise	54%	49%	49%	45%
Problems with stress	43%	44%	42%	45%
High fat in diet	47%	43%	41%	34%

HRA Overall Risk Levels	2010	2011	2012	2013
Very High (76-100)	2%	2%	2%	0%
High (51-75)	53%	50%	54%	53%
Moderate (26-50)	39%	42%	38%	46%
Low (1-25)	6%	6%	5%	0%

HRA: Weight Related Risk Factors (% at Risk)	2010	2011	2012	2013
Obese	24%	24%	18%	19%
Overweight	34%	35%	40%	33%
Underweight	1%	1%	1%	1%
Recommended weight	42%	39%	41%	46%

While this scorecard shows data through second quarter of 2013, you can report as frequently as needed, or as frequently as data becomes is available. Timing of when the scorecard is created is important. If you are meeting with senior leaders or a wellness committee (semi-annually), for example, be sure to incorporate the most up-to-date statistics as you can. You may want to schedule your meetings to accommodate when the best available reporting can be delivered.

If you were to use this Wellness Scorecard example to evaluate the current state of this company's wellness programs, you would see a reduction in the number of obese individuals in the Weight Related Risk Factors and a positive flow of health risks as measured by the Overall Health Risks category. You could then compare these results to potentially seeing a reduction in the number of "high dollar claimants" in your medical plan which often drives a significant portion of your claims dollars.

During an annual benefits planning meeting, you could present the data from your scorecard to recommend a change in your incentives strategy to drive higher participation rates in Healthy Lifestyle Coaching program, or recommend a communications campaign to raise awareness around the benefits of having a diet with more fruits and vegetables.

In actuality, this company changed its incentives strategy to reward more for participation in both the Metabolic Syndrome screenings and Health Risk Assessment for both employees and spouses whereby medical premiums would be reduced to prior year levels, and provide additional incentive for passing the Metabolic Screening.

Measuring the Value of Wellness Program Investment

A widely accepted, primary goal of wellness programs is to reduce health care costs. However, there are a number of other goals (arguably equally as important) that an organization may claim are reasons why they should offer wellness programs:

- Increasing employee relations and morale
- Supporting a competitive benefits package that attracts and retains employees
- Increasing productivity

Industry journals and newsletters are filled with case studies and articles illustrating the value of targeted wellness programs which support the full spectrum of population health.   These studies and reports have attempted to scientifically collect data, measure and calculate the economic value and impact of their specific wellness programs.

But if you're not preparing to deliver a case study or publish a doctoral thesis, how do you justify the financial investment (either for a new program or to continue an existing one) in workplace wellness programs? This will always be a challenge for organizations to manage. Benefit professionals often need to report back to the Chief Financial Officer, HR leader or an executive team on whether the spend on wellness programs has been worth it the investment.

Early in my career when I was initially recommending that my company offer a disease management program, the health plan we were partnering with offered a suite of wellness programs. They shared their book-of-business Return on Investment (ROI) to help us evaluate whether to move forward and offer their wellness programs. Book-of-Business represents the activity of ALL customers who use their programs. The one promise that could not be made was to get an ROI of our own. We had to make a decision based upon a number of inputs including benchmarking data and the expert opinion of our benefits consultant at the time.

As I've learned, there are a number of challenges as to why it's so hard to measure ROI:

- It takes many years to accumulate the data
- You need a system of measurement to collect and track the data, which is complex
- There are no widely accepted methodologies for calculating economic outcomes for wellness programs
- Tools to actually measure are unavailable or difficult to access
- Difficult to compare one organization to another
- Your organization may be too small of a population size (not credible) to make any reasonable predictions. One or two large claimants can skew your results
- Methodology in the tool includes certain assumptions which can change over time

- You don't have control over a number of assumptions or "inputs" used to determine the outcomes
- Price of health care (which also can vary by geographic region)
- Who gets hired to work for your organization (turnover rate can influence your general population)
- Changing priorities within your organization influence your ability to engage employee participation rates in wellness programs.
- Argument can be made that ROI measurements provided by health vendors may be simplified and skewed because they have a vested interest in showing good numbers

Nevertheless, companies want to know whether your wellness programs are having an effect.

Are Companies Measuring ROI

The International Foundation of Employee Benefits (IFEBP) plans reported in 2012 that only 19 percent of companies surveyed actually measure the return on investment in their wellness programs. [11]   Often, companies rely upon their health plans, third party vendors and benefit brokers/consultants to measure ROI for them.

The IFEBP survey also discovered a number of common characteristics of "ROI Achievers," those companies who measure ROI.   Of those who measured ROI, each of them:

- Offered comprehensive, full array of health/wellness offerings
- Effectively communicated to their population
- Provided incentives to motivate engagement
- Have a broad health/wellness strategy

Of all of the companies who actually measure the outcomes of their financial investment in wellness programs, 84.2 percent of them are actually achieving ROI. This means that their investment is paying off. According to their standards, the investment in wellness programs is having a positive economic effect.

Benefits Received from Wellness Investments

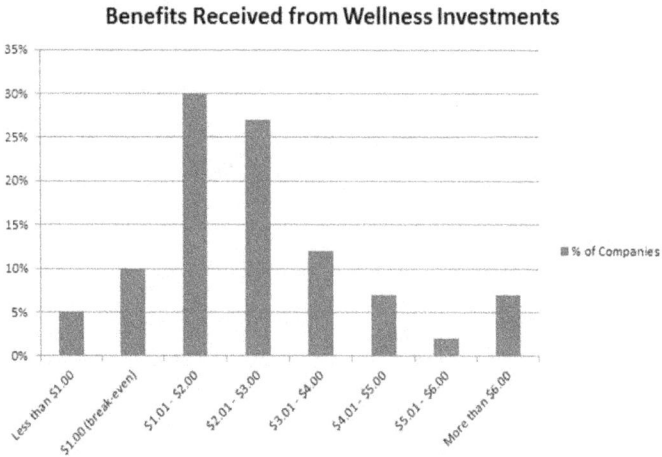

Source: *IFEBP, A Closer Look: Wellness ROI 2012*

What is Return on Investment (ROI)

Return on Investment is often expressed as the monetary benefit (or savings) associated with a program divided by the cost of that program expressed as a percent. Let's say you sponsored a wellness challenge where teams of employees competed against other teams for most weight lost and most exercise minutes. As a result of the program, a total BMI point reduction of 540 was attained (as reported by the online tracking tool). Based upon industry standards of what one BMI point is worth ($202), your ROI would be about $109,000 less any upfront investment and administrative costs.

BMI is highly correlated with medical and pharmaceutical claims costs. A reduction in an individual's BMI by one point is associated with a $202.30 savings in medical and pharmaceutical claims costs over a one-year time period. [12]

I would raise caution for accepting the savings amount in this example as gospel. The assumption is each of the participants continues to keep their weight down and continue to exercise at the same rate for an entire calendar year. Most likely, the wellness contest ran for a 12 or 16 week period. You and I know how hard it is to be consistent when it comes to our health.

The ROI measurement in this example is helpful, if not directional, in support of offering a similar wellness challenge again. But you need to be careful in claiming that you've just saved nearly $109,000. Down the road, you may have that "one in four persons" at risk for cardiovascular disease suffers a stroke putting them into a long-term care facility.

If you are interested in measuring your companies "ROI," you can try using a ROI calculator offered by WellSteps.

http://www.wellsteps.com/roi/resources_tools_roi_cal_health.php

Application of Industry Studies to Support Return on Investment

As I mentioned earlier, it's not easy to develop meaningful ROI for a variety of reasons. If you are hard-pressed to show proof that workplace wellness programs work, there are reliable industry sources that measure the effectiveness of workplace wellness programs.

Meta Study on Worksite Health Programs

In the *American Journal of Health Promotion*, March/April 2012, Larry Chapman, MPH published his Meta Evaluation of Worksite Health Promotion programs which provided a systematic look at the quality and summary results of the literature on the financial impact of workplace health promotion programs (62 studies). I like to equate this economic review as a "smoking gun" of sorts. This study was actually an update to an earlier published study that reviewed literature on the financial impact a number of years prior. The results of his 2012 study validated the same results found in 2006: workplace health promotion programs support a return on their investment.

Summary of Findings

- For every dollar invested, the average return was 5.56 (1:5.56)
- 25.1% reduction in sick leave
- 24.5% reduction in health care costs
- 40.4% reduction in workers compensation costs
- 24.2% reduction in disability management costs

Rand Corporation Study on Effectiveness of Disease Management Program

In a study funded by PepsiCo, the Rand Corporation conducted an assessment of over seven years of PepsiCo's Healthy Living wellness program. The PepsiCo wellness program includes numerous components such as health risk assessments, on-site wellness events, lifestyle management, disease management, complex care management and a nurse advice phone line. The study evaluated the experiences of more than 67,000 workers who were eligible for the disease management or lifestyle management programs.

Researchers found that the disease management program reduced costs among participants by $136 per member per month, or $1,632 annually, driven by a 29 percent drop in hospital admissions. Among people who participated in both the disease management and lifestyle management programs, the savings were $160 per month with a 66 percent drop in hospital admissions. Overall, researchers found that efforts to help employees manage chronic illnesses saved $3.78 in health care costs for every $1 invested in the effort.

The results are published in the January 2014 edition of the Journal of Health Affairs.

Industry Recognitions

One great way to help validate an organization's efforts supporting a culture of health is through industry recognitions. Whether it's through a local health organization, a business group or a national industry leader, you'll find significant learning opportunities going through the application process for industry recognition of your organization's wellness programs.

The spectrum of recognitions may run wide, but each are typically founded upon solid principles and metrics that can serve as guidelines to help you develop and enhance your workplace wellness program, potentially taking it to the next level. While applying for an industry recognition may be a "nice to have," they can tangentially have positive effects on recruitment and retention efforts for your organization.

American Heart Association   Fit-Friendly Company Recognition Program
(http://ffc.heart.org)

The Fit-Friendly program recognizes employers who champion the health of their employees and work to create a culture of physical activity and health in the workplace. Worksites can apply on an annual basis for the basic Gold level recognition and/or their advanced Platinum level recognition. In addition, worksites can apply annually for a unique "Innovation" award. These are awarded to worksites that creatively implement programs to promote physical activity in the workplace and/or community. Recognition is valid for one year and worksites must renew annually.

National Business Group on Health
(www.businessgrouphealth.org)

The BEST EMPLOYERS FOR HEALTHY LIFESTYLES® awards program acknowledges and rewards National Business Group on Health member companies demonstrating creative, comprehensive and effective solutions that improve employee health, productivity and well-being.

The BEST EMPLOYERS FOR HEALTHY LIFESTYLES® awards program, now in its seventh year, serves as a means of sharing successful interventions, strategies and services, and illustrates best practices that can be emulated by other companies. The focus and specific criteria for the award are updated annually with evidence-based standards that reflect the evolving field of workplace well-being and health promotion.

HERO Scorecard (www.the-HERO.org)

The HERO Employee Health Management (EHM) Best Practices Scorecard is designed to help organizations learn about EHM best practices – and discover opportunities to improve their programs and measure progress over time. The Scorecard can be of practical and strategic use. It's a free online survey that teaches you about EHM best practices as you complete it – and provides you with an instant assessment of how your program stacks up to others in the national Scorecard database.

WELCOA Well Workplace Awards
(www.welcoa.org)

To advance an aggressive national worksite wellness agenda, WELCOA has developed the Well Workplace Awards initiative. The Well Workplace Awards initiative is driven by a rigorous set of criteria which recognizes organizations that have built successful results-oriented wellness programs as defined by WELCOA's Seven Benchmarks. Their application contains the criteria that must be addressed in documenting program accomplishments in a completed twelve-month program cycle.

Business Council of Fairfield County (CT)
Healthy Workplace Employer Recognition
http://www.businessfairfield.com/

The Healthy Workplace Employer Recognition program is an initiative of The Business Council of Fairfield County's Wellness Roundtable. The Business Council of Fairfield County's Healthy Workplace Employer Recognition Program showcases some of the best practices and breakthrough thinking for effective promotion of employee health and wellness. Employers from throughout New England are eligible to apply for one of three levels of recognition.

The Greatest.com   Healthiest Companies
(http://greatist.com/health/healthiest-companies)

Employers who make The Greatest.com list of
Healthiest companies are making the 9-to-5 a
happier, healthier place every day. That means
providing workers with benefits such as on-site
fitness classes, child care centers, healthy subsidized
meals and fun perks like regular happy hours,
company retreats and open, light-filled office
spaces. Each company is listed according to rank,
although each size category is a separate division
(meaning that the top ranked in the "huge
companies" field is not comparable with the top
ranked entry in "tiny companies"). While each of the
companies described have exemplary health
benefits, The Greatest.com look for businesses with
perks that go truly above and beyond what's
expected.

Reporting Program Results: Executive Report

At least annually, I recommend you create a concise and thorough executive level report on the prior plan year wellness program activity and define what your future plan year goals and objectives will be. Creating this report can satisfy a number of needs:

- Report top line program results and challenges to senior level decision makers
- Document program activity for auditing purposes
- Justify recommendations / changes based upon prior plan year activity
- Promote your own value as a benefits professional (toot your own horn)

The format for this report can come in many forms. The PowerPoint deck is a common way to share information. The format lends itself well for presentations, especially when viewed online. It forces you to be brief, concise and to-the-point.

Creating a "white paper" type executive summary can serve as a stand-alone document which can be easily circulated, shared and posted on an intranet or other document sharing platform.

Regardless of the format you use, include sections that will help to reinforce and remind your audience about program offerings and any program accomplishments.

Executive Summary
The overview summary should be one to two paragraphs describing wellness programs like a "year in review" abstract. Highlight accomplishments, challenges, financial investments/ROI, then go into detail in subsequent sections.

Program Definition/Strategy
Define overall approach, strategy, objectives. List what you hope to accomplish

Programs Offered
Remind audience what programs were offered, under what conditions, the timeframes, who was eligible, vendors who supported the program and incentives available. Include an updated timeline on your three to five year plan of topline programs offered, plan to offer and what you plan to evaluate to be offered.

Financial

What were the financial investments made? Include a high level summary of medical/health plan claims data or total costs. Are you able to show ROI or estimate results/impact of programs? What type of benefit communications investment did you make? Did you see any positive results from communications investment?

Challenges

What prevented you from accomplishing your objectives? Were there any cultural or organizational issues? Did your vendor fully support? This is where you can make assessments and insights into lessons learned, as well as request new resources, funding and gain acceptance/input on objectives. Is it time to recalibrate what you thought you could accomplish?

Accomplishments and Goals

Great place to insert your wellness scorecard, especially if it includes goals. Otherwise, provide a list of programs offered with at least one to two years of data annualized. Use a simple chart with columns by year showing activity and participation levels reached. Upon evaluation, define what your future goals will be for the coming year.

Metrics and Evaluation in Summary

Common and successful approaches for managing workplace wellness programs need to be shared, recognized and supported. While most companies are offering varying degrees of wellness programs, many are not actually measuring outcomes or the health results of a program. For example, are you seeing a reduction in cholesterol scores after implementing a nutritional counseling program? Only 37 percent of companies responding to a Global Wellness Survey conducted by Buck Consultants in 2010 indicated that they measure outcomes.

"Insufficient resources" ranks at the top of the list of reasons why outcomes are not measured. The Buck Global Wellness Survey identified a number of other key reasons why outcomes are not measured, including how 36 percent don't even know how to measure outcomes. This latter point suggests a skills gap that can be remedied.

In the end, it's important to be realistic about achieving ROI or some other financial goal if your wellness programs are new, and especially if you haven't been collecting the necessary data all along.

Keep in mind the following when it comes to measuring workplace wellness program effectiveness:

- Take a long-term view

- Identify goals to measure

- Initially focus on participation rates

- Compare medical claim utilization rates yearly

- Verify methodology to measure

Health Care Reform and Wellness Programs

If you plan to manage workplace wellness programs, you will have to make sure your programs are compliant with a number of laws and requirements. The good news: if you use a third party vendor like an insurance company or administrator, they are already administering compliant programs. If you're not using a third party to manage your wellness programs, then you have a little work to do. My best recommendation is to get a reliable and trusted source to give you sound advice and direction to ensure you're being compliant. Your benefit consultant, broker or legal counsel should be able to help.

If you're using the health risk appraisal offered by your medical plan, it's reasonable to expect that their tool and system is compliant. A number of years ago, questions related to family history around genetics were removed from the appraisals, for example, soon after GINA (Genetic Information Nondiscrimination Act of 2008) was passed. Most were compliant with GINA well-before the law went into effect.

However, if you're planning to offer financial rewards that involve healthy outcomes, tobacco cessation and wellness program participation, then you should take a breather and collect your thoughts first and become very intimate with the regulations.

The Patient Protection and Affordable Care Act builds upon existing wellness program policies and creates new incentives to promote employer wellness programs. The Act also encourages opportunities to support healthier workplaces through appropriately designed, consumer-protective wellness programs in group health coverage. The visibility and availability of rewards for wellness programs will only increase adding to the need to ensure that incentive programs are not misaligned with your wellness program goals and thereby, not in compliance.

Many employers use incentives to encourage participation in their wellness programs. Wellness program incentives take a variety of forms. Examples include cash and gift cards, reductions in health care premiums and items such as t-shirts and pedometers. In the U.S., wellness incentives must not be discriminatory as specified by the Americans with Disabilities Act (ADA), the Health Insurance Portability and Accountability Act (HIPAA), the Genetic Information Nondiscrimination Act (GINA), FMLA and state laws.

For wellness programs being offered in connection with an employer group health plan for policy or plan years beginning on or after January 1, 2014, incentives up to 50 percent of premiums are allowed for non-smokers, and incentives up to 30 percent of premiums are allowed for participation in a health-contingent wellness program, as long as the HIPAA nondiscrimination requirements are met. This applies to any group health plan whether Fully Insured, Self-Insured, large or small group, grandfathered or non-grandfathered.

Premiums in this definition are the same annual premiums that a health plan charges for a fully-insured medical plan. Or in the case of self-insured, premiums would be the "hypothetical" premiums your benefits consultant would develop after taking into account your claims budget, administrative fees and stop-loss insurance.

While it's always recommended you read and understand the rules for yourself and obtain sound advice from your plan advisor, attorney, broker or consultant, wellness programs are allowed under HIPAA's nondiscrimination rules as long as they follow several conditions:

First, none of the conditions for obtaining a reward under a wellness program can be based on an individual satisfying a standard related to a health factor, or if no reward is offered, the program complies with the nondiscrimination requirements (assuming participation in the program is made available to all similarly situated individuals).

For example:
1. A program that reimburses all or part of the cost for memberships in a fitness center.
2. A diagnostic testing program that provides a reward for participation rather than outcomes.
3. A program that encourages preventive care by waiving the copayment or deductible requirement for the costs of, for example, prenatal care or well-baby visits.
4. A program that reimburses employees for the costs of smoking cessation programs without regard to whether the employee quits smoking.
5. A program that provides a reward to employees for attending a monthly health education seminar.

Second, wellness programs that condition a reward on an individual satisfying a standard related to a health factor must meet five requirements described in the final rules in order to comply with the nondiscrimination rules.

1. The total reward for all the plan's wellness programs that require satisfaction of a standard related to a health factor is limited — generally, it must not exceed 30 percent of the cost of employee-only coverage under the plan. If dependents (such as spouses and/or dependent children) may participate in the wellness program, the reward must not exceed 30 percent of the cost of the coverage in which an employee and any dependents are enrolled.

2. The program must be reasonably designed to promote health and prevent disease.

3. The program must give individuals eligible to participate the opportunity to qualify for the reward at least once per year.

4. The reward must be available to all similarly situated individuals. The program must allow a reasonable alternative standard (or waiver of initial standard) for obtaining the reward to any individual for whom it is unreasonably difficult due to a medical condition, or medically inadvisable, to satisfy the initial standard.

5. The plan must disclose in all materials describing the terms of the program the availability of a reasonable alternative standard (or the possibility of a waiver of the initial standard).

Follow this link to read the final Department of Labor regulations for Wellness Programs offered by the Departments of Treasury, Labor and Health and Human Services.

http://www.gpo.gov/fdsys/pkg/FR-2013-06-03/pdf/2013-12916.pdf

If you're not interested in reading through the several hundred pages, the Frequently Asked Questions About the HIPAA Non-discrimination Requirements presented by the U.S. Department of Labor, Employee Benefits Security Administration may be more your speed.

http://www.dol.gov/ebsa/faqs/faq_hipaa_ND.html

Conclusion

When it comes to workplace wellness, you don't have to reinvent the wheel. Refine best practices to support your strategy and objectives. Learn from your experience.

There are a number of universal "lessons learned" that all organizations can benefit from when planning out their workplace wellness strategy. The Integrated Benefits Institute published a Workforce Health and Productivity case study review in 2011 of nine different companies who were identified as leaders in addressing health and productivity.

These are the lessons in common they shared:

Just Get Started
Create a plan
Data is critical
Engage leadership
Develop support systems
Communicate to the front lines
Engage employees

Wellness Program's "X-Factors"

We can probably all agree upon the value of WELCOA's Seven Benchmarks, National Wellness Institutes Cycle of Wellness, Population Health Management, Behavioral Economics and a host of other best practices as critical strategies for helping to manage a successful workplace wellness program.

But when you peel back the proverbial onion, what are the "invisible" success factors of workplace wellness programs? Is there a key resource, a critical step, an administrative process, a communication solution, technical insight or some other type of unsung hero-like event that made the program work? If it wasn't for that certain "X Factor," would your program have been successful? You may not realize what that X-Factor is until after the program is over and you've completed an evaluation, so keep your eyes open.

One of the key ingredients for engagement in workplace wellness is empowerment. Employees must be aware of what they need to do to participate in a program. It's not enough to just announce a new initiative, new program or provide the link to the website where employees can learn more. We need to simplify and provide the critical steps that someone must take to engage and participate in a wellness program. Often much is assumed about the ability of our audience to comprehend what we are asking them to do.

X-Factor Case in point

I believe we take for granted the technological proficiency level of people. Online systems and tools assume everyone is from Generation Y having grown up playing video games and are accustomed to using computers. (If it wasn't for my son, I probably wouldn't have setup the Wi-Fi on my flat screen television.) The majority of wellness programs require some type of interaction with an online system through the internet.

If you're not technologically savvy, it can be easy to miss a step or even give up early because the process isn't intuitive to you. If you can effectively convey those critical steps to your employees, you can achieve a higher rate of participation, engagement and overall happiness (especially when a reward is attached). Otherwise, people will tune-out and that's not a fun alternative. There are enough distractions in the world causing some to not engage in your wellness program, don't give them any more reasons.

New Skills for the Effective Workplace Wellness Professional

As I mentioned in an earlier chapter, an overwhelming majority of senior executives feel that there is a skills gap in the U.S. workforce. Soft skills such as communication, critical thinking, creativity and collaboration are at the core of the gap.

For workplace wellness and benefit professionals to be successful at managing programs, they need to possess a wide range of skills. In addition to being subject matter experts on workplace wellness and benefits, such professionals also need to be proficient in a number of additional competencies, or "X-Factors" to be successful. These include:

Communications
Collaboration
Project Planning
Financial Savvy
Technical
Networking

Heraclitus, a Greek philosopher of the late 6th century BC, observed, "No man ever steps in the same river twice, for it is not the same river and he's not the same man." The river in this metaphor is workplace wellness strategies and tactics. We pull from the river what we need and what has worked before, applying it to our own organization's goals and objectives, creating a best-fit solution. As a result, the river gets replenished and revitalized with new and improved practices for the next person who comes along. Our job is to figure out how to best apply those previous experiences to the situation at hand enabling us to replenish the wellness river for others to benefit from.

Resources

In addition to this book, there are other valuable resources available to help you manage workplace wellness programs.

Industry Resources

Chapman Institute (www.chapmaninstitute.net)

Employee Benefit News
(http://ebn.benefitnews.com)

International Foundation of Employee Benefit Plans
(www.IFEBP.org)

Kaiser Foundation (http://kff.org)

National Wellness Institute
(www.nationalwellness.org)

Society for Human Resource Management Professionals (www.shrm.org)

Wellness Council of America (www.WELCOA.org)

WellSteps (www.wellsteps.com)

World at Work (http://worldatwork.org)

LinkedIn groups

Healthy Enterprise

Wellness 2.0

Wellness is a Business Strategy

Benchmarking Surveys
If you participate in a study, you can often receive an executive summary or a full report of the results for free.

Aon Hewitt
Buck Consulting
Kaiser Foundation
Mercer (Marsh & McLennan Company)
National Business Group on Health
PwC
Towers Watson

Footnotes

1 Robert Wood Johnson Foundation-funded State
Health Access Data Assistance Center (2012)
http://www.rwjf.org/en/about-
rwjf/newsroom/newsroom-
content/2013/04/number-of-americans-obtaining-
health-insurance-through-an-employ.html

2 Benz Communications, *Inside Benefits
Communications Report* (2012)

3 MetLife's *8th Annual Study of Employee Benefits
Trends* (2013)

4 Benz Communications, *Raising the Bar*; MetLife
Benefits Symposium (2013)

5 Daniel H. Pink, Drive: The Surprising Truth About
What Motivates Us (Riverhead Books, 2011)

6 Towers Watson / NBGH Employer Survey on
Purchasing Value in Health Care (2013)

7 OptumHealth, *Wellness in the Workplace Research
update* (2012)

8 Deci E, Koestner R, Ryan R. *A meta-analytic review of experiments examining the effects of extrinsic rewards on intrinsic motivation. Psychol Bull.* 1999; 125:627–688.

9 Zoeller, Kristie, CEBS, Benefits Magazine, October 2012. International Foundation of Employee Benefit Plans.

10 Aon Hewitt, *2013 Health Care Survey*

11 International Foundation of Employee Benefits plans, *A Closer Look: Wellness ROI. 2012.*

12 Edington, Dee, *Association of Healthcare Costs With Per Unit Body Mass Index Increase,* American College of Occupational and Environmental Medicine (2006).

13 David Kindig and Greg Stoddart. What Is Population Health? American Journal of Public Health March 2003: Vol. 93, No. 3, pp. 380-383.)

14 Creating and Sustaining a Culture of Health and Wellbeing at Johnson and Johnson. World Congress 7th Annual Employer Health and Human Capital Congress, Washington, D.C. February 8, 2012.

15 Jeanne Meister, Forbes.com: Leadership. *Gamification: Three Ways to Use Gaming For Recruiting, Training, and Health & Welfare.* May 21, 2012.

About the Author

William Pokluda is a CEBS-recognized professional with over 20 years of experience in employee benefits supporting the culture of health. He received his bachelor's degree in Psychology from William Paterson University and his MBA from the University of Connecticut. He also earned the Certified Workplace Wellness Specialist (CWWS) designation from the National Wellness Institute, and the Global Mobility Specialist designation from Worldwide ERC. For three years in a row, he helped his employer earn the Healthy Employer Recognition (Platinum level) from the Business Council of Fairfield County. He lives and works in Fairfield County, Connecticut.